Tech-Savvy Reading Promotion

Tech-Savvy Reading Promotion

A Toolbox for Librarians and Other Educators

Nancy J. Keane

LIBRARIES UNLIMITED™

An Imprint of ABC-CLIO, LLC

Santa Barbara, California • Denver, Colorado

Library of Congress Cataloging-in-Publication Data

Names: Keane, Nancy J., author.
Title: Tech-savvy reading promotion : a toolbox for librarians and other
    educators / Nancy J. Keane.
Description: Santa Barbara, CA : Libraries Unlimited, an Imprint of ABC-CLIO,
    LLC, [2019] | Includes index.
Identifiers: LCCN 2018057295 (print) | LCCN 2019005143 (ebook) |
    ISBN 9781440868511 (ebook) | ISBN 9781440868504 (paperback : acid-free paper)
Subjects: LCSH: Reading—Aids and devices. | Reading—Technological
    innovations. | Reading—Computer-assisted instruction.
Classification: LCC LB1050 (ebook) | LCC LB1050 .K378 2019 (print) |
    DDC 372.4028/4—dc23
LC record available at https://lccn.loc.gov/2018057295

ISBN: 978-1-4408-6850-4 (paperback)
        978-1-4408-6851-1 (ebook)

23 22 21 20 19   1 2 3 4 5

This book is also available as an eBook.

Libraries Unlimited
An Imprint of ABC-CLIO, LLC

ABC-CLIO, LLC
147 Castilian Drive
Santa Barbara, California 93117
www.abc-clio.com

This book is printed on acid-free paper ∞

Manufactured in the United States of America

*This book is dedicated to my family who put up with the hours
spent writing and exploring new apps and my excitement when
I found new ones that I just couldn't stop talking about.
My children: Aureta and Alex
My grandsons: Aiden and Jordan
And to the memory of my mother, Aureta, who instilled the love of
reading and writing in me at a young age. One of my earliest
memories was bringing my wagon to the public library
and filling it up with new stories and new lives to live.
My mother and I spent hours at the library choosing
our books and hours during the week reading them.*

Contents

Acknowledgments

Thank you to the many teachers and students who were always ready to let me practice on them. There were many apps that students tried out to be sure they were kid-friendly. The kids were always happy to tell me when they loved an app. And quick to tell me when they didn't! And my assistant, Felecia Sargent, who never rolled her eyes when I said, "Hey, let me show you this new app! Let's try it!"

A big thank you to my editor, Barbara Ittner from Libraries Unlimited. This book would never have been written without her encouragement.

Introduction

"Reading is a foundational skill for learning, personal growth, and enjoyment. The degree to which students can read and understand text in all formats (e.g., picture, video, print) and all contexts is a key indicator of success in school and in life. As a lifelong learning skill, reading goes beyond decoding and comprehension to interpretation and development of new understandings" (American Association of School Libraries, 2007, 2).

Students in middle and high school spend less time reading for pleasure than elementary students. Guthrie and Davis (2003) examined the decline of independent reading at the middle school level and found that as students go through middle school, opportunities to self-select reading materials decreased. In a study of summer reading programs, Gordon and Lu (2010) found that low-achieving students reported they did not think they had free choice in selecting reading materials. Higher-achieving students reported more control over reading choice. Krashen (2004) reported that 51 out of 54 students studied allowed free choice of independent reading books and did as well or better on reading tests as students engaged in traditional reading instruction. Stairs and Burgos (2010) found that when students were given time during the school day to read and select a book, students became more interested in reading, read more often, and reported more pages read. Miller (2012) found that allowing her students to self-select gave them power and buy-in and removed the opportunity to refuse to read at all. Greaney and Clarke (1975) found that the increases gained through sustained silent reading appeared to last years after the program ended.

When students were encouraged to self-select their reading materials, Krashen (2004) found that students sometimes did not select books appropriate to their reading level or understanding. Students needed help choosing books for independent reading. Students don't always know which books may interest them nor understand how to find out. They may need the help of adults to find just the right book that will keep them interested. But librarians and teachers don't always have the time and resources to help children select their reading books. Parents may not have the expertise to help them. We can use technology to help them select books in a variety of different ways.

Using book promotional tools helps students:

- Become aware of which books are available for them to read.
- Be informed about which books may interest them. If they are lovers of a particular genre such as fantasy, book promotional tools can share other fantasy books for them to choose from.
- Develop an awareness of the many books that match their interests. Many times children automatically head for fiction books for free reading. They may not be aware of nonfiction titles that they will enjoy.

Teachers and librarians who work with children know how they react to promotional materials. When introduced to a variety of books, children will usually find a book that speaks to them and makes them want to pick it up to read.

We now have more tools than ever to find books that kids will enjoy—print guides, online websites, databases, etc. And now there are even apps that can guide young readers in finding books they will love. It is estimated that by 2020, there will be more than 5 million apps in the Apple App Store. There is no way for anyone to be able to use all the apps or even keep up with the number being created. Many apps begin as free apps and may become paid apps when they become popular. And many apps disappear every day. Some of my favorites have disappeared in the time it has taken to write this book.

Many of the apps that appear each day start out with a particular use in mind. Whenever I explore a new app, my first question is "How can I use this for book promotion"? I find many apps that may be used to create the same promotion (posters, videos, podcasts), and it is up to personal choice as to which is used. Some video editors make excellent videos for use on TV or YouTube. They allow extensive editing capability and special effects for when you want a high-quality video. But others can make quick videos to use on the fly when production value is not the top priority. Still others allow for real-time live video streaming. The one you choose is based on how you will use the final product and how comfortable you are with using the app. It is hoped that you will try a few apps in the chapters to find your favorites.

Goal of This Book

The goal of this book is to introduce you to information and instruction on the use of a variety of free apps that can be used in book promotion routines. The emphasis is on the use of *free* technology apps in the book promotion program. Many of the apps included in the book may have upgraded paid accounts that offer more bells and whistles than the basic free accounts. When there are paid accounts, emphasis is on the basic free accounts. Examples of the use of the apps is intentionally simple to illustrate how even quick, basic promotions may be used.

As apps come and go, so do their capabilities. The information in this book is up to date at the time of printing—however, a few apps may have changed, changed to a paid app, or disappeared completely.

How to Use This Book

The book is divided into four chapters that group the technology—Visuals, Videos, Audio, and Resources—to help find books and tools to use in your reading program. There is no need to use the book sequentially. Use the chapter and the technology that you need to enhance your book promotion. Every recommended app is available to use for free. There may be a paid account as well, but the description in this guide focuses on features of the free account. Some of the apps require the user to request an educator account. Effort was made to include programs and apps that work on a variety of devices. Each app mentioned gives the user information as to what device it works on. When desktop apps are recommended, it is because they can be used online and do not need to be downloaded onto the computer, although there are a couple of exceptions because of the quality of the apps.

Chapter 1 introduces programs and apps that can be used to create visual book promotion projects. These can be used in flyers, on web pages, or printed promotional materials.

Chapter 2 focuses on video production. These apps can be used on web pages or any promotion involving video. From quick videos that can be used immediately to talking avatars to fully edited videos, there is an app for every occasion.

Chapter 3 provides information on audio promotions. From podcasts to radio advertisements, audio is a great choice for book promotion.

Chapter 4 includes many resources that can be used to develop your book promotion. From literary quotes, to YouTube channels, to book widgets, there are many ideas for you to use.

Whether it is creating a poster to introduce an event, or creating a video of a child recommending a book, there are unlimited ways that you can promote reading. There are no right or wrong ways to build your program. It depends on your population and your comfort around technology. You also do not need to use each app in isolation. Mashing up apps and using several for one project keeps things interesting. Build it and they will come.

Further Reading

American Association of School Librarians. (2007). *Standards for the 21st Century Learner*. American Association of School Librarians. Retrieved from http://ala.org/aasl/sites/ala.org.aasl/files/content/guidelinesandstandards/learningstandards/AASL_LearningStandards.pdf

Gordon, C. A., & Lu, Y. (2008). "I hate to read—or do I?": Low achievers and their reading. *School Library Media Research*, 11.

Greaney, V., & Clarke, M. (1975). A longitudinal study of the effects of two reading methods on leisure-time reading habits. In D. Moyle (Ed.), *Reading: What of the Future?* (pp. 107–114). London: United Kingdom Reading Association.

Guthrie, J. T., & Davis, M. H. (2003). Motivating struggling readers in middle school through an engagement model of classroom practice. *Reading & Writing Quarterly*, 19(1), 59–85. doi:10.1080/10573560308203

Ivey, G., & Broaddus, K. (2001). "Just plain reading": A survey of what makes students want to read in middle school classrooms. *Reading Research Quarterly*, 36(4), 350–377. doi:10.1598/RRQ.36.4.2

Krashen, S. D. (2004). *The Power of Reading: Insights from the Research*. Westport, CT: Libraries Unlimited.

Miller, D. (2009). *The Book Whisperer*. Hoboken, NJ: Jossey Bass.

Miller, D. (2012). Creating a classroom where readers flourish. *Reading Teacher*, 66(2), 88–92.

Stairs, A. J., & Burgos, S. S. (2010). The power of independent, self-selected reading in the Middle Grades. *Middle School Journal*, January, 41–48.

Figures

CHAPTER ONE

Visuals

Word Clouds

A word cloud is a visual representation of text. Also called tag clouds, they provide readers with a powerful way to look at text. The word cloud contains pieces of text that are put into a list. The size or weight of the word in the final word cloud is determined by how many times the word appears in the text. The more times a word is included, the larger the word will be in the word cloud. Tags, or words, are usually single words.

There are hundreds of uses for word clouds in education, and librarians can use word clouds for a variety of book promotion activities. Any text can be turned into a word cloud and then printed, embedded into a web page, or added to social media.

Here are some ideas for using word clouds in book promotion:

- Create a word cloud of an author's work. The word cloud can use just the titles of books or use the genres of the books to show what genres the author writes in.
- Create a word cloud that stresses titles in a genre. Add several titles of books into the tag list, and create the word cloud from there.
- Create a word cloud that highlights the most important aspects of a novel.
- Create a word cloud for book shelves that draws attention to the titles in the section. Use several titles from one book shelf or one section of shelves.
- Create contests for children to guess the book represented in the word cloud. You can emphasize character names to help the kids figure out the book.

Before beginning to add text to a word cloud, determine the purpose of the word cloud. If you are using a word cloud to promote all of the works of an author, first determine if you want to use the titles of the books or key words for each book. You can paste text into the create box or type the words you would like to have represented. For those words that are emphasized, type the word many times to create a larger font. The words that need to be smaller should appear fewer times in the create box.

Here are some examples of word cloud generators and how they work:

Wordle
http://www.wordle.net

Wordle is a web-based application that is free to use. You do not need to be signed up to use the service. Wordle does not work with all browsers. The browser must have Java installed. You must have an up-to-date Java installed in order for it to work.

- Click on Create New to begin your Wordle.
- Paste in text or type in text to be used in the word cloud. The size of the word in the final Wordle is based on the number of times the word is used in the text. To emphasize words, repeat them over and over.
- Click on Go.
- Your Wordle is now displayed.
- To change how it looks, choose Randomize.
- You can also change the font, layout, and color.
- Save to the public group (if logged in).
- You can also open the final Wordle in another window and save the image.

Microsoft Word

Microsoft Word can be used to create word clouds. Word requires an add-in be added to the program. The add-in is free and easy to install. You only have to install it once.

To add the Word cloud add-in to Word:

- Open Word.
- Click Insert on the ribbon.
- Click Get Add-ins.
- Click Store.

- Search for word cloud add-in.
- Click Add to add word clouds to your program.

To create a word cloud using Word:

- Create a new document. Choose blank document.
- Click on Insert > Add-in > My add-ins.
- A task pane will appear on the right side of the document.
- In the blank document, paste text or type text to begin your word cloud.
- When all the words are entered, choose:
  - Font.
  - Colors.
  - Layout.
  - Case.
  - Max words.
  - Size of word cloud.
  - You might want to remove common words so you can check that box.
  - Select text.
  - Click on Create Word cloud button.
- A preview of the word cloud will appear. If you do not like the word cloud, you can change the formatting options and regenerate it.
- When you are happy with how the word cloud looks, right click on the word cloud to print it out or to save.

Other word cloud generators have different features, so try out a few to see which one works best for you.

Microsoft PowerPoint

Microsoft PowerPoint can be used to create a word cloud directly into your presentation. You will be able to add the word cloud to your presentation and/or save it to your files.

You will need to add the Word Cloud Add-in to your copy of Power-Point in order to use the word cloud maker. To add the word cloud creator to PowerPoint:

- Open PowerPoint.
- Click Insert on the ribbon.

- Click Get Add-ins.
- Click Store.
- Search for word cloud add-in.
- Click Add to add word clouds to your program. You will not need to add it in each time you want to use it.

To create a word cloud using PowerPoint:

- Create a new document. Choose blank slide show.
- Click on Insert > Add-in > My add-ins.
- A task pane will appear on the right side of the document.
- In the blank document, paste text or type text to begin your word cloud.
- When all the words are entered, choose:
  - Font.
  - Colors.
  - Layout.
  - Case.
  - Max words.
  - Size of word cloud.
  - You might want to remove common words, so you can check that box.
  - Select text.
  - Click on Create Word Cloud button.
- A preview of the word cloud will appear. If you do not like the word cloud, you can change the formatting options and regenerate it.
- Right click on the word cloud to print or save it into your presentation. To add the word cloud to your slide, use the copy/paste command.

When using PowerPoint for a book promotion, think of using a word cloud to summarize your presentation. PowerPoint presentations can be saved as a video and used on your web page or social media. Or you can set PowerPoint to play in nonending kiosk mode to play in your library or classroom.

ABCYa! Word Clouds
http://abcya.com/word_clouds

ABCYa! is a free web-based application that is also available for iOS and Android. It is free to use to create your word cloud.

- Open ABCYa word cloud.
- Click on Create New.
- Paste or type in your text into the text box.
- Click Create.
- You can randomize the results and change the layout, color, or font.
- Layouts include shapes such as stars, hearts, diamonds, etc.
- Once your word cloud is finished, you can click Save or Print.

Google Docs
http://docs.google.com

Creating a word cloud using Google Docs is similar to how it is done in Word. You can use Google Docs on the desktop at http://docs.google.com. It is also available on iOS or Android devices. You will need to create a Google account.

- You will need to add the Add-on from the Add-ons available.
- Create a new document.
- Choose Add-ons and select Word Cloud.
- Paste in the words you want to be in your word cloud into the text box.
- You will find the generated cloud on the right.
- Right click to save or print the word cloud.

The word cloud can be used in a Google Docs document, or you can save the word cloud to use with other applications or on social media. The word cloud can be used in Google Slides or even on a Google Form.

TagCrowd
http://www.tagcrowd.com

TagCrowd is a web-based application that can be used to create free word clouds. You do not need to create an account or sign in.

- You do not need to log in to use TagCrowd; simply paste or type your text into the box.
- Click on Visualize.
- You have the chance to do some editing before you finalize the word cloud.
- When you are finished, you can save, create an embed code, print, or save as a PDF.

You can use the embed code to put the word cloud into your web page or use on social media.

Tagul
http://tagul.com

Tagul is a free web-based application that is easy to use to create a word cloud.

- Create your free account to get started.
- You can upload, paste, or type your text into the box.
- Choose the shape, color, and background for your word cloud.
- Download or share your word cloud on social media.

Tagxedo
http://tagxedo.com

Tagxedo is a web-based application and does not work with all browsers. You will need to use a browser that supports the newest Java plug-in.

- You will need to create an account to log in.
- Click on the Create button to begin constructing your word cloud.
- Upload, paste, or type your text into the box.
- You can change shapes, themes, fonts, and direction of your text to suit your needs.
- When finished, you can print or save your word cloud.

Use your word cloud to add to other applications, or use it alone.

WordClouds
http://wordclouds.com

WordClouds is a web-based application that can be used in your browser.

- You do not need to log in; simply go to web page and click File.
- Upload, paste, or type your text into the box.

- Choose size, shape, flatness, theme, color, and font.
- You can link words in the cloud to web pages by inserting the URL. This will include all the words on the web page, so be careful using this option.

Using a word cloud app is ideal when using a word cloud on a web page and highlighting a section of the library, an author, or a genre.

Poster Makers

Posters are a good way to promote books and reading. Posters can be used in a variety of ways to grab the attention of children. The most popular way is using posters to decorate the walls of the library or classroom. Or even posting them in the stalls of the bathrooms. And that is why librarians and educators have used them in the past, relying on commercially produced posters, often freebies from the publishers. But commercial posters can be pricey, and it takes time to order and receive them. And posters might not be available for the books you want to promote, particularly if it's a classic title or even a current release that isn't a blockbuster. You can also use local teachers and children to star in your own created posters. Today, you can produce your own posters, customized to fit the needs of your students and patrons. But posters can also be embedded into web pages or shown on screens in the library or classroom or even produced in smaller sizes for children to take home or used as prizes for contests.

Ideas for using posters in book promotion are as follows:

- Use posters to promote library events, including author visits and book clubs.
- Use posters to promote reading challenges.
- Use a character to promote a book.
- Create a poster showcasing an author's work or series of books.
- Create a poster of a scene from a book.
- Create a poster of books in a genre.
- Create a poster of the state book award nominees to entice students to read them.
- Posters are a good way to promote thematic books or new books.

There are many free poster makers that are available that can help you create an interesting poster that will be enjoyed by your patrons.

Block Posters
http://www.blockposters.com

This is a free, web-based poster maker that will take a photo and turn it into a large poster. The poster will be printed in 8½" ×11" sections, which is the size that most local printers can handle. Print out all the sections and then assemble them into a large poster. There are edges around each sheet that allow slight overlapping of sheets to make assembly easier.

- There is no need to create an account or to log in.
- Click on Create Your Poster.
- Upload your image.
- The poster will print on multiple pages.
- Crop your poster to include the parts of the photo you want to make into a poster. You do not need to use the entire picture.
- Customize your poster by editing:
  - Number of sheets of paper.
  - Paper size. The most common paper size is 8½" ×11", but you may have a printer that can print a different size.
- Click on Create My Poster.
- Click on Download. Your poster will download as multiple PDF sheets.
- Print out all the sheets.
- Assemble the sheets to create your large poster.

Adobe Spark
http://spark.adobe.com

Adobe Spark can be found on the web as a web-based app. It is also available as an iOS app or an Android app. You can sign up for a free account using your Google account or Facebook account, or create your own account using your e-mail. (See Figure 1.1)

Steps to create a poster:

- Once you've created your account, log in.
- Click on the green plus sign and choose Post.
- Choose a template or start from scratch.
- Choose the size of the photo (there are different sizes depending on where you plan to post the picture or if you are doing a poster). Some

Figure 1.1   Adobe Spark Post

templates are optimized for specific sites such as YouTube, Facebook, etc.

- Upload you own photo or search for photos in the Adobe database. Choose the photo(s) you want to use and then click Next.
- Choose a design and double click to add the text.
- You can change the elements of the Post using the buttons in the app.
- Elements that can be edited include Pallet, Orientation, Filters, Animation, Fonts, Size, and Shape.
- When you are finished, click Share.
- Your work can be saved as a poster, video, or live photo.

Use posters to liven up walls or even social media. Colorful posters catch the eye and can convey your message about reading.

Recite This
http://www.recitethis.com

Recite This is a free website where you can create beautiful posters comprised of quotes. (See Figure 1.2)

- When you go to the page, a text box will open.
- Enter your quote into the text box.
- Select your style from the choices along the bottom.
- Click Create.
- You can click on Save. You can post to social media, download the image, or e-mail the poster to yourself as an attachment.
- This site is used by many people, so you may have to wait in a queue for your poster to render.

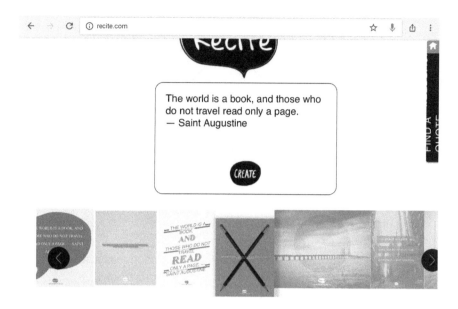

Figure 1.2   Recite This

Quotations from popular authors about the joys of reading or what reading has meant to them are a good way to spark children's desire to pick up a book.

PosterLabs

PosterLabs is a free app that is available for iOS and Android. It is easy to use and creates nice posters. There is no need to have an account or to sign in. (See Figure 1.3)

- Click New.
- Select photos from your camera roll. You may use up to five photos for each poster.
- Click New Poster.
- Select style. There are several styles to choose from. Several of the styles are only available in the paid app, but the free app has lots to choose from.
- Click on the text to write your own.
- Click on Save. It automatically saves to the camera roll.
- Share to social media if wanted.

This is an easy app to use to create a poster or a collage to use on various sites. You can also print it out to use as a poster.

Keep Calm App

This is a free app for iOS and Android. There are advertisements that pop up on this app, but it is easy to use.

To create a visual:

*   Click on the dice icon to change the background and cycle through the posters.
*   Choose a poster to use.
*   Change the text by clicking on the word to select the text and typing in your text.

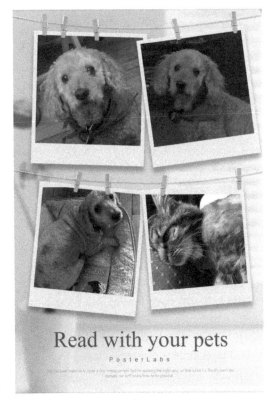

Figure 1.3 Poster Labs

*   Click on the graphic to eliminate it, or change it with one in the app.
*   Change the text style by clicking on the A icon.
*   Change the background color by clicking on the paint brush icon or the grid icon.
*   When finished, click on Upload icon.
*   You can share the poster on social media, or Save to your camera roll.

The style of these posters is immediately recognizable. They can be whimsical or serious.

Photo Editors

Photo editors can be used to enhance photos as well as to change them or combine them to create book promotion items. The altered photos have many uses in book promotion.

Photos can be used for:

- Brochures that advertise new books, books by genre, or thematic book lists. You can have a genre of the month brochure or poster that showcases one genre each month.
- Displays for book events that promote reading and books.
- Social media posts advertising books.
- Newsletters used for book promotion.
- Shelf talkers or shelf wobblers.

There are many photo editors on the Internet. Play with a few and decide which one you like. Some are very simple to use and offer just a few options for altering a photo. Some are powerful editors with lots of bells and whistles. Choose the app that is appropriate for your project and abilities. The apps mentioned here are free to use. The free apps may be limited and have fewer options than their paid subscription.

Shelf talkers: A shelf talker is a sign that attaches to the shelf, making it pop out to the children. It helps interest the students in the book advertised.

Shelf wobbler: A shelf wobbler is similar to a shelf talker. The difference is there is some interaction or movement included. You can purchase plastic clips that allow the shelf wobbler to move or wobble. This attracts the eye and will entice the children to stop and look.

Flip book shelf hanger: A flip book shelf hanger is a small flip book that is laminated and held together with a ring. There can be several books promoted that are shelved near where the flip book shelf hanger will be placed. (See Figure 1.4)

To create either a shelf talker or wobbler, you simply need to have text and/or photo printed that can be mounted. There are many programs that do a good job of creating the display photo.

Some of the more popular photo editors are:

Figure 1.4   Flip Book Shelf Hanger

PicCollage
http://pic-collage.com

PicCollage by Cardinal Blue Software is a free web-based platform. It is also available as an app in either iOS or Android. (See Figure 1.5)

* Create an account and log in. You can use your Facebook account or e-mail to create an account.

* Get started by choosing your layout. Grids, Freestyle, or Cards are available.

Figure 1.5   PicCollage

* Choose photos from your camera roll or file.

* In the upper right, you will see a blue box with the number of pictures you have chosen. When you are finished choosing pictures, click the check mark.

* Now you will see your photos on the screen. You can move your photos around, change the layout, add more photos, add stickers (not all that are available are free), add text boxes, or animate your picture.

* When you are finished with your collage, click Done.

* You can upload your photo to social media or save it to your camera roll.

PicCollage has many uses. A picture is an eye-catching way to get children excited about a book.

PicMonkey
https://www.picmonkey.com

PicMonkey is a web-based application. It is also available as an iOS app. To begin using PicMonkey,

* Choose from:
    * Blank canvas.
    * Edit a photo.
    * My hub.
    * Upload photos.

To edit a photo to use in book promotion,

- Click on Edit a Photo.
- Choose photo from camera roll.

You can then share, edit, add to, or delete.
Edit your photo using:

- Crop.
- Adjust.
- Effects.
- Touch up.
- Text.
- Draw.
- Stickers.

Add text then click Done.
Save to your camera roll.
Share to social media.

PicMonkey is an easy-to-use app that is versatile enough to make good photo collages to use in your program.

BeFunky
http://www.befunky.com

BeFunky is a free photo editor that is web based. It is also available on iOS and Android. BeFunky allows you to edit photos, create collages, and add text to photos. Backgrounds can be added as well as a variety of photo effects including blur, sharpen, change orientation, black and white, vintage tone, and others.
To use BeFunky:

- Click on the app.
- Upload your photo from your camera roll or your Facebook account, or take a picture to use.
- Click on Edit to crop, sharpen, blur, change orientation, etc.
- Click on Effects to choose black and white, vintage tone, etc.
- Click on Frames to add a frame.
- Click Apply to save changes.
- Click Save. You can save to your camera roll or social media.

You can use the photo from your camera roll to add your photo to other applications.

Flipsnack
http://flipsnack.com

Flipsnack is a web browser app that can be used to create an online flipbook. It easily transforms PDF files into a digital flipbook. You will need to sign up for an account using your Facebook account, your Google account, or your e-mail.

To create a flipbook:

- Go to http://flipsnack.com.
- Sign in.
- Click Upload Your PDF Files.
- Upload your files (or just drag and drop PDF and JPG files)
- Click Next.
- You can customize the appearance of your publication by changing:
  - Language.
  - Background colors.
  - Full screen.
  - Next.
  - Title.
  - Description.
  - Category.
- The Editor allows you to add:
  - Links.
  - Text.
  - Images.
  - Video.
  - Shapes.
- Publish. You can share your photo on social media or get an embed code to use.
- Click to copy a direct link to the flipbook.
- You will need to upgrade to the premium account to download.

Digital flipbooks can be used in a variety of ways. They can be added to social media or web pages to showcase a set of books. Use photos from an author event to showcase the event. Online brochures can easily be created using Flipsnack.

Gimp
http://www.gimp.com

For those Photoshop users looking for something similar, the answer may be Gimp. Gimp is a powerful photo editor. It is a free open source editor that can be used for editing photos and drawings and converting image format. It is cross platform. You will need to download to your computer.

Meme Creators

The word "meme" is short for memetics, which is the study of commonly repeated content. A meme is usually a humorous or satirical piece of content. It can be a photo and text that pairs a ridiculous photo with a witty caption.

Memes are a good way to promote books and reading. Memes can be used in a variety of ways to grab the attention of children. But memes can also be embedded into web pages or on social media.

Here are some ideas for using memes in book promotion:

- Use memes to promote library events such as author visits and book clubs.
- Use memes to promote reading challenges such as reading contests and book trivia.
- Use a character to promote a book.
- Create a meme of a scene from a book, but be sure it is not misleading or gives away the key part of the book.
- Create a meme of books in a genre.
- Memes are a good way to promote thematic books or new books.

There are many good meme creators that are available to help you create an interesting meme that will be enjoyed by your patrons.

ImgFlip
http://www.imgflip.com/memegenerator

The most popular meme generator on the web is ImgFlip. This is available as a web-based app and includes many photos that can be used in your meme.

To create a meme using ImgFlip:

- Click on Create.
- Choose the image that you want to use either from the web page, or upload one of your own.
- Enter your caption using text boxes.
- Click Generate Meme.
- Save the image to use in your promotion. You can save it to your files.

The images in this web page are used in many memes. They are recognizable, which can be a plus. Or they may have been overused. Grumpy Cat is part of the collection.

Kapwing
https://www.kapwing.com/meme-maker

Kapwing is available on the web to use as well as an app for iPhone and Android. (See Figure 1.6) To create a meme using Kapwing:

- Go to the web page.
- Upload the picture you want to use for your meme.
- Choose a template to use for your meme.
- Enter text or emojis to use in your meme.
- Choose the text options: Font, Size, Color, Alignment.
- Click Create.
- The meme is uploaded to the Kapwing website and processed.
- When the meme is ready, download to your files.

Photoshop Mix

Photoshop Mix is an easy meme generator. It is available for both iPhone and Android devices. The app is simple to use but has some advanced features that allow you to layer up to 10 items. Follow these steps to edit a photo:

- You will need an account. Log in or create an account. You can use your Google or Facebook account or create an account using your e-mail address.
- Be sure all images you are planning to use are saved in your camera roll or files.

Figure 1.6   Kapwing

- Click the plus sign to start a new composition.
- Click image and choose your first image to use.
- Click the plus sign to add more layers such as:
    - Images.
    - Text.
    - Background.
    - Color.
- A special template is used for meme generation.
- When finished, save your meme to your camera roll or files, or share it to social media.

Image Chef
http://www.imagechef.com

Image Chef is a web page that allows users to create memes using templates from the site. You need to have an account to save the memes. Templates include billboards, street signs, newspaper headlines, flags, sports jerseys, signs, license plates, buttons, holiday themes, and much more. The web page can be used for free. The iPad app costs $1.99 to download.

To use Image Chef:

- Go to web page http://www.imagechef.com.
- Create a free account. You will need to sign in to save your work.
- On the main page, look through the myriad of choices of templates that you can use.
- Choose a category and look through the templates.
- Choose a template to use it.
- The image will be on the left, and the text box will be on the right.
- Replace the text with your message.
- Click Preview.
- If you are happy with how it looks, save it to My Stuff or e-mail a copy to yourself. You can also save your photo to social media.

If you want to use your own photo rather than one from the site:

- Go to profile.
- Click on Upload Photo.

- Crop to fit selection box.
- Click OK.
- Click Use This Photo.
- Pick a Stage to use.
- Tint the photo if desired.
- Add your text.
- Save to My Stuff, e-mail, or send to social media.

Image Chef is used by librarians and teachers in their book promotion efforts. Memes are a great way to add humor to web pages or social media sites. They can be used to share book suggestions or events of interest. You can use memes for motivational photos as well.

There are many other meme generators on the web and available as apps on iOS and Android devices. In addition to meme generators, many multiuse apps can be used to create memes. Apps like Canva and Adobe Spark have built in meme generators. Other apps such as Google Slides and Microsoft PowerPoint can be used to produce memes.

Infographics

The word "infographic" comes from combining the words "information" and "graphics." An infographic uses pictures and words to show information. Infographics represent information in a way that makes it easily understandable to children and are especially good for at looking at complex data in a visual way.

Infographics are a great way to grab the attention of children. They are visual and make the children think a bit about the books. Infographics can be used in a variety of ways to promote reading to children.

Here are some examples of ways to use infographics in your book promotion:

- Infographics can be embedded into web pages or shown on screens in the library.
- Use infographics to promote library events such as author visits and book-related programming.
- Use infographics to promote reading challenges.
- Use a character to promote a book. The character can give a book talk for the book.
- Create an infographic of an author's work. The infographic could show a scene from a book.

- Create an infographic that stresses titles in a genre. Characters can discuss a genre and recommend books from that genre.
- Create an infographic of the state book award nominees to entice students to read them.
- Infographics are a good way to promote thematic books or new books.
- Library metrics can be displayed using infographics to encourage students to read more. The metrics can be broken down by class or grade to encourage children to want to do better than another class.

Before beginning to create any visual, determine your purpose. Do you want to emphasize a program, a book, general reading promotion, or other ideas? Once you have determined your purpose, begin to construct a storyboard. Rough out how you want the visual to look. You can then create your infographic.

There are many good infographic makers available that can help you create an interesting visual that will be enjoyed by your patrons.

Easelly
http://www.easel.ly

Easelly is a free, easy-to-use infographic creator that is web based. An iOS app also can be used. Easelly offers a paid account option that adds more features, but the free account is a good choice for basic needs.

Here are steps to create an infographic using Easelly:

- Create an account. You can log in with your Google account or create an account with your e-mail address.
- Log in to the account.
- Explore Public Visuals to see what others are creating.
- You can use one of the Public Visuals as a template or click the Plus sign to start from scratch.
- Choose objects, background, shapes, or text from the bottom menu.
- Hold and drag each element onto the page.
- You can upload and place images of your own.
- To save, click the Save icon and add a title to your infographic.
- You can also share the infographic to social media sites or create an embed code to put the infographic on a web page.

Easelly has a variety of built-in templates that make it easy to create an infographic. If you do not want to use one of those, you can start from scratch and create your own design. When promoting books, you can use a photo of the book cover as your background.

Piktochart
https://piktochart.com

Piktochart is a free infographic creator. It can be used on the web. It is also available as an app for iOS and Android. It is useful for presentations and posters as well as infographics. You need to create an account to use Piktochart. You can sign in with Google or Facebook or create an account using e-mail.

To create an infographic, log in and choose Infographic.

- Click on Create New.
- You can look through the templates and use one of them if it fits your needs.
- If you do not want to use a template, you can choose a Blank page and create your own.
- Upload any graphics you want to use. Piktochart accepts several different image types.
- Click on the photo to add it to your blank canvas.
- You can resize and reposition your images.
- Using the icons on the left, you can add text, shapes, graphics, lines, backgrounds, charts, maps, and frames.
- When the infographic is completed, you can Save, Share to social media, download, or create an embed code to use on a web page.

Canva
http://www.canva.com

Canva is a free infographic creator available on the web as well as iOS and Android. It has professional layouts to help you design stunning graphics. Canva is also a good app to create presentations and social media graphics.

To use Canva, you need to sign up to create an account. You can use either your Google account or your e-mail to create an account. You will be asked to indicate if you are an educator, a business, a nonprofit, or a charity. (See Figure 1.7)

Here are steps to create an infographic using Canva:

- Click on Create a Design.
    - There are several designs to choose from, including post-card, flyer, poster, and social media templates.
    - Click Find Templates. Search the Infographic Templates. There are more than 50,000 templates to use.
- When you find the template you want to use, click on it.
- In the workspace, you can choose:
    - Layouts.
    - Elements (Photos, Grids, Frames, Shapes, Lines, Illustrations, Icons, and Charts).
    - Text.
    - Backgrounds.
- You can upload your own photos.
- You can resize as needed.
- Share to people, social media, link, or embed.
- You can also download the infographic.

Snappa
http://www.snappa.com

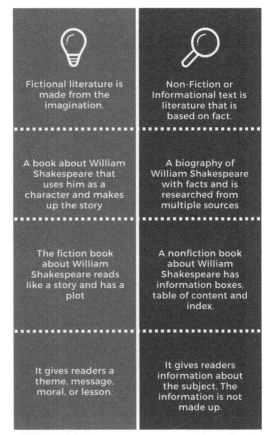

Figure 1.7   Canva

Snappa is a free, user-friendly web app that can be used to create info-graphics. You need to create an account using your e-mail. The free Basic

Figure 1.8 Snappa

Account includes limited templates and five downloads per month. (See Figure 1.8)

To create an infographic, follow these steps:

- After you sign in, click on Infographics.
- Choose the infographic template that best fits your needs.
- Use the buttons to add Background, Effects, Text, Graphics, and Shapes.
- You can upload and use your own photos.
- You can layer elements and move them around via drag and drop.
- The infographic can be resized if needed.
- The free account does not permit Save from the page, but you can download the infographic.
- Download the infographic.
- You can share your infographic to social media. The free account limits direct linking to two social media accounts. The ability to share directly to social media is a plus for this site.

Infogram
http://www.infogram.com

Infogram is a free, web-based, easy-to-use infographic and chart maker. There are more than 1 million images and icons,

35+ charts, and 550+ maps in the paid version of Infogram. The free Basic Account is more limited, but you can upload your own images and icons.

You need to create an account to use Infogram. You can use your Google, Facebook, Twitter, or LinkedIn accounts, or use your e-mail to create your account.

In addition to infographics, Infogram has templates for reports, charts, dashboards, maps, social media, and more. You can use the account to create more than infographics.

To create an infographic, follow these steps:

- Click on the Infographic Template.
- Choose the template you plan to use and click on it. There are only a few templates available in the Basic Account.
- Choose Public or Private. If you are using the Basic Account, you can only choose Public.
- Click Create.
- The tools on the left side of the workspace allow you to add:
  - Chart.
  - Map.
  - Text.
  - Graphics (you can upload your own).
  - Shape.
  - Media.
  - Layout.
  - View.
- On the right-hand side, you can:
  - Add page.
  - Change theme.
  - Project size.
  - Project background.
  - Share button.
- When you have finished your infographic, review your work and make any changes needed.
- Click Share.

For Basic Account:

- Public.
- Add title.

- Add description.
- Social media.
- Create an embed code.
- E-mail a link directly to the infographic.

Infographics can be used in so many ways in book promotion. Try a few of the ideas and see how they fit into your program.

Comic Strips

Comic strips have been a favorite genre for children for years. Be it the Sunday comics in the newspaper or graphic novels, comics connect with visual learners. You just need to watch children gathered around the graphic novel section of a library or bookstore to know how popular they are and how enticing. It is no wonder that advertising companies are using this format to sell products. And it is just as easy to promote reading and books using comics.

Comics can be used in a variety of ways to promote reading, as detailed below. Remember, comics can be as short as one panel or fill up a whole page. They can be embedded into web pages or printed and used as posters.

Here are some ideas for using comics in book promotion:

- Create a comic of an author's work. The comic could show a scene from a book.
- Create a comic that stresses titles in a genre. Characters can discuss a genre and recommend books from that genre.
- Create a comic for book shelves that draws attention to the titles in the section.
- Use comics to promote library events such as book clubs or author visits.
- Use comics to promote reading challenges.
- Create a comic of the state book award nominees to entice students to read them.
- Comics are a good way to promote thematic books or new books.
- Create comic bookmarks.

Before beginning to create a comic, determine your purpose. Do you want to showcase a program, a book, general reading promotion, or other ideas? Once you have determined your purpose, begin to construct a storyboard. Rough out how you want the comic to look. How many panels will you have? Will this be a quick one-to-three-panel comic for a web page or a longer comic? Who will be the characters? Will they be human or animal or other? Decide on the text and any other details needed. You can then create your comic.

There are many good comic makers that are available that can help you create an interesting comic.

MakeBeliefsComix by Bill Zimmerman
http://makebeliefscomix.com

MakeBeliefsComix is a web-based application that is straightforward to use. You do not need to be signed up to use the service. The program will create a simple comic up to nine panels long using preset characters.

- Click Create.
- Choose how many panels you want in your comic. You can have up to nine panels.
- Choose your character(s). Many characters are built into the app. Scroll through until you find the one you want.
- You can change the direction and size of the character.
- Add dialog balloon and insert text. You can edit the font and size of the text.
- Add more characters or change the look of your character until you have all the panels completed.
- Review your comic.
- Save—print, save to your files, or e-mail the comic.

MakeBeliefsComix is a good choice to make simple comics. The characters are included, and the process of creating a comic is not complicated.

There is no iOS or Android app for MakeBeliefsComix, but you can install an icon as a link on your mobile device to be able to access the site quickly. To add the MakeBeliefsComix icon as a link on your mobile device, follow these steps:

- The process involves a couple of steps from your web browser: In Safari, tap the Share/Send icon.
- Scroll to see the Add to Home Screen button (a rounded square icon with a plus in it).
- Tap Add to Home Screen to add the icon to your home screen.

- In Chrome and Internet Explorer click on the more menu (three dots) on the upper right of the browser.
- Tap Add to Home Screen to add the icon to your home screen.
- Go to your Home Screen and launch MakeBeliefsComix!

ToonDoo by Jambav
http://www.toondoo.com

ToonDoo is a web-based application that is free to use. You can make a comic that has one to four panels. You need to create an account to use ToonDoo. Follow these steps:

- Sign in once you have created an account.
- Click on the ToonDoo Maker button.
- Choose a layout. You can use horizontal layouts or vertical layouts and choose one to four panels.
- Choose a character from the ToonDoo app by simply dragging and dropping the character into the panel.
- Place and size your character using the buttons at the bottom.
- You can change the emotion and posture of the characters. They can be happy or sad or even angry.
- Choose background by dragging and dropping from the built-in choices.
- Choose props if you want them by dragging and dropping them into the scene.
- Tool buttons at the bottom of the screen allow you to edit the individual elements: Clone, Flip image, Rotate image, Send to front/back, Change emotion or posture of character, Add text bubbles and add text. If you want to copy a panel, click in the box in the upper right of the panel.
- Save the finished comic.
- Choose to let others edit or even buy your comic.
- Publish to the world, keep it private, or send it through an e-mail.

After your comic is published, you can print it or save it to use in social media or on a web page.

Other comic generators have different features, so try out a few to see which one works best for you. Some have more features than others. Decide what features are important to you in generating your final comic.

StoryboardThat
http://www.storyboardthat.com

StoryboardThat is a web-based comic maker that is a free site to use. Simple drag-and-drop features make it easy to create your comic. The program walks you through the creation. You need to sign in to save your comic. You can sign in using your Google account, your Facebook account, Twitter, etc.

To create a storyboard comic, follow these steps:

• Click on Create a Storyboard.
• The web page will open up to blank panels with scenes that can be used at the top of the page.
• The scenes are grouped by home, school, transportation, historical sites, and more.
• Click and drag the scene you want into one of the boxes.
• You will be prompted to edit the scene for picture rotation, crop, filters, sky color, and more.
• You can then add another scene into the next panel until all the panels have scenes.
• You can add more panels if you need them.
• Click on Characters to add characters to the panels. The characters include children, historical figures, monsters, and more.
• You will be able to edit the pose and the features of the characters.
• Click Textables to add speech bubbles and thought bubbles. Type the text in the box on the edit screen.
• Other elements that can be added include shape, web icons, science icons, and more.
• When the comic is finished, click on Save.
• Add a title and description.
• You can then download, copy, delete, print, or create an embed code.

The free account only allows two saves a week. If you want to do more, you will need to upgrade to a paid account.

Witty Comics
http://wittycomics.com

Witty Comics is web based, and you will need to create an account to save comics.

- Go to the website.
- There is a three-panel layout. The prebuilt scenes and characters are below the panel.
- Click on the scene beneath the panel. There are many to choose from. Simply click on another to look at scenes and change scenes.
- Add narration to the scene to explain what is going on.
- To add characters, click on the thumbnails beneath the panel. There are multiple characters in different poses and emotions.
- Add the words they are saying by typing them in the text box beneath the panel. You can choose the type of dialog bubble you want to use.
- Add a title for your comic strip.
- When you are finished, log in and save your comic strip.

Witty Comics is simple to use and to save for your use in other applications. It is limited to comic strips with three panels.

Surveys and Polls

Children love to have a say in what they read. When deciding on leisure reading, they should be given a choice. When choosing independent reading, children use a variety of techniques to decide on what to read next. If you want to know what they are thinking, the best way is to ask.

Surveys and polls are a quick and easy way for children to tell others what they want to read. A survey is generally used when you have multiple questions you want answered. A poll is used when there is just one question that may have several answers.

Surveys or polls can be used in a variety of ways to promote reading:

- Surveys or polls can be embedded into web pages or shown on screens in the library. Some can even be added to presentations to allow for real-time polling.
- Use surveys or polls to promote library events. Or get thoughts on which events are of interest. Give children a say in what types of reading promotions they want to attend.
- Use surveys or polls to promote reading challenges.
- Create a survey or poll of the state book award nominees to track students' interest in them. Children can vote on their favorites.
- Surveys or polls are a good way to promote thematic books or new books.

Google Survey
http://forms.google.com

It is simple to create a survey in Google Forms. Using Google Forms makes it easy to compile the results by linking the form to a spreadsheet.

- Go to http://forms.google.com and log in with your Google account. Google Form is also available on iOS or Android devices.
- Choose New Blank Form or you can use a built-in template. Or you can go to Google Drive. Click New → More. Choose Blank Form or from a template.
- Name the form and change the background color if you wish.
- Add a description of what you are asking the children in the survey.
- Add questions:
  - Click Untitled Question and enter your question.
  - Choose question format. There are many to choose from including multiple choice, short answer, paragraph, check box, dropdown, file upload, and linear scale.
  - Add response options. You can require respondents to answer a question or let them skip a question.
  - To add additional questions, click Add Question.
  - You can reorder, delete, or edit questions.
  - You can add an image to the question if you wish.
  - You can link to a YouTube video if desired.
- Choose form settings. You can collect e-mail addresses of respondents, limit the number of responses, or allow respondents to see results of the survey.
- You can share the survey by sending e-mails to those you want to respond. You can also embed the survey into a web page.
- The responses are collected on a Google Form.

Doodle
http://doodle.com

You will need to sign up on Doodle, but you can log in with your Google account or your Facebook account, or create a new account using your e-mail address. Doodle is also available on iOS or Android.

To create a poll:

- Click the plus sign to begin a new poll.
- There are two types of polls available:
  - Time poll—asking participants to choose a time they are available.
  - Text poll—asking participants to choose a text response.
- Add a title to the poll.
- Select options.
- Optionally, you can add a location and/or a note.
- Select the settings you wish to use:
  - Yes/no option—participants need to answer yes or no for each choice.
  - Hidden poll—only the owner of the poll can see the results.
  - One vote—if you want participants to only vote once.
  - Limit votes per option.
- Click Create.
- Invite participants using e-mail or social media.
- Answers are tallied in the app.

Dotstorming
http://dotstorming.com

Dotstorming is a free, simple-to-use poll creator. The free account is now limited to one board, but you can reuse that board or pay for an upgraded account. It uses a sticky note format to add information, and then participants can vote for choices that are offered. The site keeps track of the number of votes for easy display.

The person who creates the Dotstorming board needs to have an account. Those who are responding do not have to sign in. They just click on Join and add their note or their vote.

To create a Dotstorming board:

- Go to the web page and log in.
- Add the topic. Create a description to let the children know what is being asked.
- You then invite participants. You are given a URL that the students can use to access the poll. You can also embed this into a web page.

Student use:

- Students click on the URL for the poll.

- Students join and add name—can be first name only or screen name.
- Students can add an idea—click on Add a Card and they can add an idea in text or images.
- Students can vote on other cards. Click the round dot on the card. You can limit how many votes they get. If they change their mind, they can vote on another card and it will delete their other vote. Students can also comment on a card.
- Once the students have had a chance to add cards, you can lock the board. This will disallow any further cards or comments but allow voting to continue.

Dotstorming can also import Pinterest boards. If you have a Pinterest board with your choices on it, you do not need to replicate it on Dotstorming. Simply import it. The thumbnails appear along with the voting option.

Poll Everywhere
http://polleverywhere.com

Poll Everywhere offers free educational accounts, but they are limited to 40 responses per poll. You can use the same poll many times but must reset the responses if they will exceed the 40 responses.

Sign up for an Educator account. Poll Everywhere can be used live and integrated into a presentation. You need to use the web-based account to create the polls, but students can use their devices to respond to the polls. (See Figure 1.9)

- To create a poll, determine what type of poll will work best for your needs.
  - Multiple choice allows your students to include several items to choose from.
  - Word Cloud—the students will respond in short text answers which will be combined to create a word cloud.
  - Question and Answer.
  - Rank order—students drag their top choice to the first position.
  - Clickable image.
  - Survey.
  - Open ended.
- Share the poll with your students. You can give them a URL where they can respond, or they can text their response from their device. Poll Everywhere creates the URL and the text number.
- The responses are anonymous.

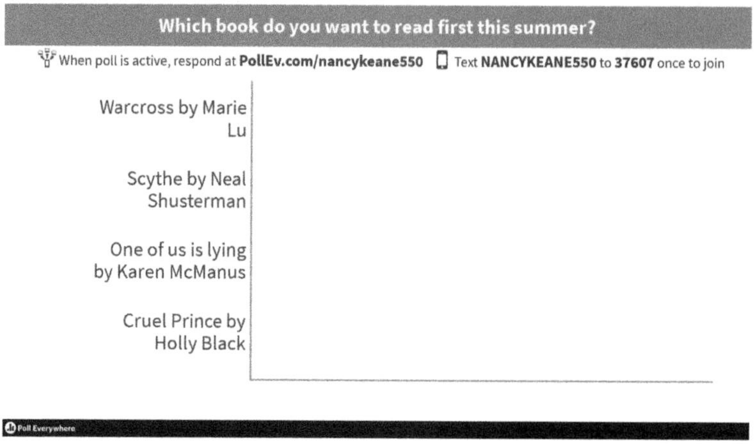

Figure 1.9   Poll Everywhere

Embedding the poll into a Google Slide:

- First add the Chrome app to your Chrome browser.
- Chrome Apps → Poll Everywhere.
- This will add Poll Everywhere to the Google Slide menu bar.
- To add a slide to your presentation, click on Poll Everywhere from the menu bar and click Insert.

SurveyMonkey
http://www.surveymonkey.com

If you are already a SurveyMonkey user, you are quite familiar with creating surveys and polls. This is another good choice for sending out surveys and polls.

To use SurveyMonkey, you can create a free account. Use your Google account, Facebook account, Office 365 account, or LinkedIn account. If you do not want to use one of those, you can sign up with your e-mail address.

After creating your profile, you can create a survey:

- Click on Create Survey.
- Name your survey.
- Choose a category from the dropdown box. Categories include Just for Fun, Events, and more.

- Click Create Survey.
- If you already have your questions written, you can copy and paste them into a survey.
- You can design your own survey or work from one of the templates.
- Once you have chosen a template, you will be brought to a sample survey with questions already created.
- You can search the question bank for questions already written or write your own.
- Once you have created all the questions, click Next, and you will be able to decide how to collect responses.
- You will be asked three questions to determine how your survey should be shared:
  - Do you have an e-mail list to use?
  - Do you want feedback from visitors on your web page?
  - Do you need help finding people to take your survey?
- You can get the weblink of the survey to share, send by e-mail, post on social media, share in messenger, embed on a website, embed in a mobile app, add data manually, or print survey.
- After you receive your answers to the survey, you can use SurveyMonkey to summarize the responses and analyze the results.

You might want to use SurveyMonkey if you have a more detailed survey to send.

Timelines

Timelines are a good way to display information in a chronological way. Timelines are particularly useful with historical fiction as well as biographies and other historical nonfiction books to connect the events in a story to events in the "real world." You can also represent the events in a book to show how they flow through the story.

Timelines are a quick and easy visual for children to understand the chronology of a story or series.

- Timelines can be embedded into web pages or shown on screens in the library.
- Use timelines to promote reading challenges. If children are interested in a particular time period in history, a timeline suggesting novels that take place in that time can allow students to discover new books that they would enjoy.

- Timelines are a good way to promote thematic books or new books. You can display a timeline of books that occur in a particular time period. For example, show books that take place during the colonial period or books leading up to World War II.
- Timelines of an author's life and influences help students understand the author's work.

Time.Graphics
http://time.graphics

Time.Graphics is a web-based program for creating timelines. The Public Account is free to use. You do need to sign in, which can be done via your Google account or social media accounts, or by creating a new account using an e-mail address. If you want more choices, you will need to upgrade to the paid account.

- Open the program and click on the Create New button.
- A timeline is prebuilt with the current date assumed.
- To add events, click on New Event. You will be prompted to add:
  - Event—add a short description of the event.
  - Date of the event.
  - Choice of event being above or below timeline. This can make the timeline easier to understand.
  - You can choose the color to designate an event. If you are using dates in the Revolutionary War, you may want to use red for British and blue for colonials.
- You can zoom in or out to make the timeline reflect a time period.
- Add photos if wanted.
- Add videos if wanted.
- Save—download, URL, or embed code.
- If you want to add your kids to be able to look at a large timeline and to see the pop-ups, it is better to use the embed code or to link to the URL. Saving a JPG will not allow the timeline to be interactive.

Timetoast
http://timetoast.com

Timetoast is a free, web-based site that allows you to make easy timelines. You do need to create an account. All public timelines are free and are available for anyone to see. If you want to create private timelines, you will need to purchase an account.

- To create a timeline, click Public Timelines.
- Click Create Timeline.
- Fill in timeline details including Title, Publish Status, Category, and Photo.
- Click Create Timeline.
- You will be able to add events using the Timeline editor.
- Click on Add Event.
  - Add the Event details.
  - Add the time span.
- Click on Add Event to add additional events.

Once you are finished, change from Draft to Public. You can share the URL or embed into a web page. You can use the timeline to create a chronology of an author's life or events that occur during the course of a book. There are many uses for timelines. Experiment with different forms and see what works in your program.

Google Slides

If you only have a couple of points on your timeline, you may want to use Google Slides. There is a built-in timeline generator. More than four events may be too hard to read. There is limited space on the slide, which makes the font smaller for each event.

To use Google Slides for a timeline:

- Open Google Slides.
- Click on Create New.
- Insert → Diagram.
- The task pane opens showing the templates available.
- Choose Timelines to choose that template.
- Edit the template to create the desired timeline. Add the events and dates in the template.
- Save your timeline. You can save it as a Google Slide, or in JPG, PDF, or other formats.

Using Google Slides to create a timeline is a good way to add a quick timeline into a slide show without having to use an external timeline creator.

Tiki-Toki
http://tiki-toki.com

Tiki-Toki is a web-based timeline generator. Tiki-Toki creates "beautiful interactive timelines" that can be shared on the Internet.

You do need to sign up for an account. Free accounts come with one timeline that includes multiple views, upload to YouTube and Vimeo, sharing with URL, and color coding stories. If you wish to create additional timelines or collaborate with others, you will need to upgrade to a paid account.

Tiki-Toki takes you through the steps in creating a timeline. You can add up to 500 events on the timeline. You can change the arrangement of the events, background color, and highlight color.

To create a timeline:

- Sign into your account.
- Click on Create New Timeline.
- Now it is time to tell your story. Click on Create New Story.
- Click on Admin in the upper right corner.
- A pop-up will appear that allows you to fill in the details.
- Choose a beginning and ending date for your timeline event.
- Enter a brief description of the event.
- Add image if desired and click paste.
- Add a video that will play when clicked by copying the URL of the video.
- Click Save.

You can share your timeline with the URL that is generated. You will also be able to embed the timeline into other applications.

Fake Texting

TextingStory: Chat Story Maker

Teens love to text. There is no doubt about that. Look around and you will even see preteens and elementary children texting on their phones. It may be a natural to use texting to tell stories. Or even promote books.

TextingStory is an easy way to create a reading promotion (thing). Two characters can have a conversation in a text chat. This can be turned into a video that can be added to social media sites or your web page.

To use TextingStory chat:

- Open the app.
- You will see a page with two characters and a blank text chat.
- Click on settings to change the names of the characters who are texting, change the colors of the text, add a photo of the character, add the typing sound, and add a title for the story.
- To create the chat, alternate between the characters by clicking on the names on top of the screen.
- When you are typing the chat, the chat is being recorded. Any corrections you make will show up in the final video, so make sure you have the text you want to use in mind.
- You can edit the chat to delete lines.
- Once the chat is finished, click Create Video.
- You can save the video to your camera roll or share to social media.

Text chats are a fun way to promote books. You can use two characters from the book to talk about relevant events to spark interest. Or you can even have your characters having a disagreement. Unless you are sure you know what you are doing, stay away from "kid-speak" in your chat. It is a real turnoff to kids to have adults try to sound like kids.

Fake Chat Story

Fake Chat Story is an app that lets you create text chats that can be turned into videos and shared. There is no need to sign in or create an account.

To use Fake Chat Story:

- Open the app.
- You are taken to a blank text screen.
- Click on a name to start the chat. To change the names of the characters, click on the top middle icon. You can change the names and add a new member to the chat.
- Alternate names to create the chat.
- The chat is being recorded as your type.
- To create another story, click on New Story and click the green plus sign.
- To edit a story, click on the blue pencil. Click on the line to edit and then edit or delete that line.
- When finished, click movie icon to create the video.

- Save to social media or your camera roll.
- Click on Stories to bring up a gallery of saved chats.

Using fake texts to promote books is a natural. Your characters can be two people talking about a book or asking for suggestions for a book. You can even use characters from the book to entice kids to learn more about the book.

Avatars

An avatar is an icon or figure representing a particular person. Avatars can be lifelike representations or cartoon characters. Avatars can be used on social media to embody a person.

There are many avatar creators on the Internet. Play with a few and decide which one you like. Some render serious avatars, some are more cartoon-like, and some even let you create yourself as a famous character.

Avatars can be used:

- To promote reading.
- To promote individual book titles.
- As a shelf talker to recommend books in the shelves.
- As a brand for an individual or a library.
- In printed materials, such as brochures and newsletters. Have your avatar introduce new books in your newsletter.
- To identify new books or specific areas of the library.
- On social media.

Be sure to check usage rights on the avatars to be sure you can use them the way you wish. Some sites have restrictions on how their avatars are used.

Avachara
http://www.avachara.com

Avachara is a free site that is very easy to use to create avatars. There is no need to sign in or create and account.

To create an avatar:

- Choose whether your character will be male or female.
- Choose the skin color.

- Choose the shape and color of the eyes.
- Choose the shape of the nose.
- Choose the shape of the mouth.
- Choose the shape and color of the eyebrows.
- Choose the hair.
- Dress up your avatar. Choose from the clothes in the app.
- Decide if the avatar will have prop items such as glasses or other objects.
- Choose wallpaper.
- Click Make Picture.
- You can save your avatar for use or post to social media.

Cartoonify
http://www.cartoonify.de

Cartoonify is a free, easy-to-use avatar generator. You can save your avatar and use it on social media. It can be used as the face of your book collection program. (See Figure 1.10)

To create an avatar:

- Open the web page.
- Choose a face shape. There are several to choose from.
- Choose a color for your avatar. You can choose realistic skin color or something else.
- Choose a mouth for your avatar. There are several to choose from.
- Choose a nose for your avatar.
- Choose the shape of the ears.
- Choose the eye color, shape, and eyebrows for your avatar. You can also add glasses if desired.
- Choose the hair color and hair style for your avatar.
- Dress your avatar. There are several outfits available to choose from.
- Choose a background. You can choose an outdoor background or choose from several others.
- When you are finished, download to save. You can also share your avatar on social media.

Use your avatar as a stand-in for you on social media and print sites. Or have your avatar be your mascot.

Figure 1.10   Cartoonify

Marvel "Create Your Own" Super Hero
http://marvelhq.com/create-your-own -super-hero

Have some fun creating your own super hero to promote books. Simply choose from the selection of super heroes. Click on the Play button, which will bring you to where you can customize your super hero. When finished, save your super hero and use it in your program.

Bitmoji
http://www.bitmoji.com

Bitmoji is free and available on the web or as an app for iOS and Android. Bitmoji is an avatar creator that takes your picture and enhances it. You can create an expressive cartoon avatar, choosing from a growing library of moods and stickers. Your avatar will be able to appear in many poses and outfits. This is a very versatile avatar creator. (See Figure 1.11)

You need to create an account to use Bitmoji. Your avatar will be saved in the app, so you can use it or change it later.

To create a Bitmoji avatar:

- Log in and choose whether your avatar will be male or female.
- Take a selfie to use or create your avatar from the choices in the app: Skin tone, Hair color and style, Eye shape, lashes, size, color, brows, Nose, Glasses or not, Jaw, Face shape, Mouth, Ears, Cheek lines, Forehead lines, Eye lines, Makeup, Body type, Outfit. Using a selfie is the easiest way to create the avatar if you want it to be an avatar of you.
- When finished, edit any of the elements as needed.
- Save.
- To use Bitmojis in a variety of poses and expressions, you will need to turn on the Bitmoji keyboard to use the different features. On a smart device, go to Settings → General → Keyboard → Keyboards → Add new keyboard → Bitmoji → Bitmoji → Allow full access.
- You can now use your keyboard to control Bitmoji. Have your avatar be happy or sad, dancing, singing, laughing, waving, riding on a skateboard or car. And

many more poses and activities. You can add stickers to the avatar such as Hello, Wow, Bon Voyage, and lots more. There are so many ways to use your Bitmoji.

Literary Maps

There are many types of literary maps that can be used in your book promotion activities. There are book maps that explain where a story takes place in the real world. There are many literary maps that illustrate fantasy worlds. Many fantasy stories are based on world building, and using a map to explain that world is a natural. Use these in your program

Figure 1.11   Bitmoji

to celebrate authors and books. These can be downloaded and used in your program as a poster or handout. They can be added to your website to add interest.

- These can be embedded into web pages or social media.
- They make great displays for the library or classroom.
- Use them in animated videos or photos.
- Use them in contests and book quizzes.
- Use them to extend the understanding of the book.

Some maps that are available on the Internet are:

The 10 Best Maps from Fantasy Books for Readers Who Like to Track Heroes' Adventures
http://www.bustle.com/p/the-10-best-maps-from-fantasy-books-for -readers-who-like-to-track-heroes-adventures-40087
Many fantasy books are built around worlds created by their authors. Maps of these worlds are often printed on the inside covers of the books. Some of the maps help explain the world of the story. And some of the maps are simply beautiful to view. You can print these out to create interest in the story.

17 Literary Maps to Explore
http://ebookfriendly.com/literary-maps-to-explore
The maps of literary places have a long history and have graced the end-papers of books for hundreds of years. These maps can help students picture the world that the characters live in during the story.

18 Literary Maps of the United States
http://mentalfloss.com/article/62975/18-literary-maps-united -states
Take a road trip through famous literary sites across the United States. There may be many sites in your own state that you can highlight. These are part of the Library of Congress's Language of the Land exhibit.

20 Literary Maps
http://entropymag.org/20-literary-maps
Here you will find maps of Treasure Island, Middle Earth, Gulliver's Travels, and many more. These literary maps help children understand the world that the characters inhabit.

6 Young Adult Fantasy Book Maps to Love
http://www.readbreatherelax.com/6-young-adult-fantasy-book-maps -to-love
Literary maps can truly be works of art. That is one reason to use them in your book promotion activities. Authors spend a great amount of time world building, and those who share those worlds with us in words and maps successfully bring us on the journey. Even maps that do not have a lot of color or pizazz can take us to a new place.

9 Awesome Literary Maps Every Book Lover Needs to See
http://www.buzzfeed.com/krystieyandoli/heres-a-look-inside-this -awesome-new-book-of-literary-maps?utm_term=.kp99Pl6xv# .bnaGRym8v
This web page gives us a glimpse of the pages in Andrew DeGraff's book, *Plotted: A Literary Atlas* (2015). DeGraff is an illustrator who has created many literary maps. Take a peek at the maps from his book.

Can You Identify the Book from Its Map?
http://www.theguardian.com/books/booksblog/quiz/2014/jun/09 /maps-books-fiction-quiz
This is a fun quiz created by *The Guardian*. There are maps from famous children's books. Each map has four titles to choose from. How well do you know these worlds?

Fantasy Books with Maps
http://www.goodreads.com/list/show/32089.Fantasy_Books_with
_Maps
This is a list collected in GoodReads that give a list of books that have maps included. Not all the books are children's books.

From Middle Earth to Hundred Acre Wood: Putting Fiction on the Map
http://www.theguardian.com/childrens-books-site/2015/nov/11
/putting-childrens-literature-on-the-map-young-adult
Literary maps take us on a journey. Sometimes we can get turned around in our heads and lose our way. Using these literary maps help us discover where we are and what is around us. This page includes maps for Middle Earth and Oz and many more.

Guide to 21st-Century Literary Maps
http://www.ncte.org/affiliates/literarymaps
Part of the National Council of Teachers of English Literary Maps Project.

Maps in Children's Books
http://www.slaphappylarry.com/maps-in-childrens-books
A collection of maps from children's books. Some are designed by illustrators, some by book designers, and some by fans. Sometimes the maps come after the book becomes popular. For instance, there was no map of Harry Potter's Hogwarts until after it became a huge hit with children. In this article, we find out a bit of the backstory of literary maps.

Literary Calendars

There are many types of literary calendars that can be used in your book promotion activities. Discover author birthday calendars, literary events, book anniversaries, and more. Use these in your program to celebrate authors and books.

- The calendars can be embedded into web pages or social media.
- They make great displays for the library or classroom.
- You can use them to celebrate an author a day.
- Use them in animated videos or photos.

- Celebrate a favorite author's birthday.
- Use them in contests and book quizzes.

Some calendars that are available on the Internet are:

Anita Silvey's Children's Book-a-Day Almanac
http://childrensbookalmanac.com

Horn Book editor Anita Silvey created her Children's Book-a-Day Almanac in 2010. She describes her site as a daily love letter to children's books. If you want to share a book every day with your kids, this is a great website to explore. Each book includes an essay with information about the books. Her website has also evolved into a book that you can purchase for everyday enjoyment.

Author and Illustrator Birthdays for the Entire Year
http://www.scholastic.com/teachers/collections/teaching-content /author-and-illustrator-birthdays-entire-year

Scholastic has put together a list of author and illustrator birthdays. There is not one for every day of the year. You can use this to give a shout-out on the morning announcements or have a weekly/monthly display. Children love looking to see who shares their birthday.

Book Your Calendar
http://www.nytimes.com/interactive/2017/books/books-calendar .html

The New York Times has put together a calendar of literary events. The calendar is not limited to birthdays of authors and illustrators. They also include information about publication dates and important days in an author's life. You can add this calendar to your Google calendar of your iOS account.

Calendar of Literary Facts
http://www.enotes.com/lit-fact-calendar

This calendar has listings for every day of the year. You will find author birthdays, death dates, and important events in literary history. The site is not limited to children's literature.

Guardian's 2018 in Books: A Literary Calendar
http://www.theguardian.com/books/2018/jan/06/2018-year-in-books

A literary calendar that looks at books, authors, and events for the year. Not all the events deal with children's literature.

Literary Holidays You Should Add to Your Calendar
http://electricliterature.com/literary-holidays-you-should-add-to-your
-calendar-b46c45bd9c45

A listing of literary influenced holidays you may want to celebrate. Jolabokaflod on December 24 is one that should be added. It translates to Christmas Book Flood. It is celebrated in Iceland, but there is no reason it can't be celebrated everywhere. On Christmas Eve, everyone opens their presents, which include books, and spend the rest of the night reading.

Mr. Schu's Book Release Calendar
http://calendar.google.com/calendar/embed?src=5n3m4522bidf
16damifeiolg7k@group.calendar.google.com

Mr. Schu is well known among children's book lovers. This is his book release calendar, so you know which books to look for on the day.

Collaboration Tools

Children love to talk about what they are reading. They love to share books with others and feel connected when they do. In-person book clubs are thriving in schools and libraries. But what about those children who may be too shy to participate? Or those who need to share immediately? Online collaborative tools can create those virtual book clubs. Children can join and can then share their thoughts at any time. Here are a few collation tools that work well with online book clubs.

Biblionasium
http://www.biblionasium.com

Biblionasium is often referred to as the GoodReads for kids. Biblionasium is an online community for children 6–13 to review and share discussions about books. The site includes reading logs and book shelves and allows parent access. It works well as an online book club for children. Librarians and teachers can add groups or classes and create logins for the children. There is no need for children to have e-mail addresses. More than one class or group can be created.

Parents' e-mails can be added to the child's account so they can participate in the discussions and the challenges, or follow what is being read. Students can record books, give them ratings and reviews, and leave comments.

Biblionasium is web based. A link to the page can be added to mobile devices. In Safari, go to the Biblionasium home page. Click the plus sign and then add to home screen. Biblionasium also integrates with Follett Destiny for a small fee.

Here are the steps involved in setting up Biblionasium:

- Go to http://www.bilbionasium.com.
- Click on Join Us and choose Teacher.
- You need to provide an e-mail address and create a password. You will need to confirm your e-mail before you can add students.
- You will receive an e-mail with a link to confirm your e-mail address. When you confirm, you will need to provide the name and address of your institution.

To create classes:

- Follow the prompt to set up a class.
- Choose a reading level system. Name your class.
- Add the students. You can create usernames and passwords.
- Once all the students are added, you can have all the logins e-mailed to you.

You will be able to create reading lists. To create a book list:

- Go to Home. Click on My Books.
- Search for a book. Click on Add to Classroom. Choose your class. Choose the list type (recommended, required, favorite). Choose which students you want to add it to.

To create a challenge:

- Set up group challenges or individual challenges.
- Set up general challenges based on genres, or add specific titles to the challenge.
- Go to Home. Click on My Challenges. Choose the New Challenges tab. Walk through prompts.

If you use Follet Destiny as a library management system, you can integrate Biblionasium for a small fee. The advantage of integrating the two is that students can look up books that are in the school library and add holds or check them out. Children love the immediate access that this gives. Also, if the library has the book, the child can go to the entry and add a book review into Destiny.

Padlet
http://www.padlet.com

You do need an account to use Padlet. The free account allows you to set up three Padlets. These can be used over and over, but if you find you need more, there are paid accounts. Log in using Google, Facebook, or Office 365, or create your own account.

To build a wall:

- Choose one of the templates or backgrounds.
- Double click to add a sticky note. You can write on the wall to explain what the children are responding to. It could be a book, a genre, or any book-related discussion.
- Save the wall and create a URL for the wall. It will be a Padlet address.
- Choose the privacy setting. Be sure to remember the URL if you hide your wall. You can password protect your wall so only children with the URL can participate. You can also moderate the comments, so you can decide if they are to be shown.
- Click to create notes; add photos and videos.
- Members of the wall can scroll through all the notes to read them.
- Share the wall through social media, use embed code, or create a QR code to share.

Children love using Padlet to share their book choices. The use of the sticky notes limits the amount of words they can use, but that limit is sometimes a positive aspect of it.

FlipGrid
http://www.flipgrid.com

FlipGrid is a free service that allows users to create short videos of their thoughts. Teachers or librarians can pose a question or start a discussion on a book for a book club, and then participants can create a video of their response right in the page. FlipGrid is free and works with iPad, iPhone, and Android.

The educator must create an account. You can log in with Google or Microsoft or create your own account. You must be 13 to set up an account. When signing up, you need to include your organization information.

- Once you are set up, you can begin by building a grid. Customize the grid with the included features. You will need to name the grid, supply the purpose for the grid, and decide how public it should be.
- Some of the features include notification and what to allow users to do, including downloading their own videos.
- You can customize the image for your grid cover. When using it for book discussion, putting the book cover on the grid helps focus the discussion.
- Activate the grid.
- Invite book club members or class to the page. They will need the code to respond.

Students will:

- Find the grid and enter the code to join.
- Create a video selfie.
- Click Record to record the response.
- Click Pause.
- Add name.
- Submit video.

Children will be able to view the videos or comments that are created by others in their class. They can comment on the videos or create their own.

Lino
http://en.linoit.com

Lino is a web-based collaborative tool that is free to use. It also works on iPad, iPhone, and Android devices. It is easy to use and allows participants to create sticky notes.

To create a sticky note:

- Create an account.
- Log in and click on Create a New Canvas.
- Choose a name for the canvas. Choose the background and privacy settings.

- Canvas will hold all your sticky notes, pictures, etc.
- Click on a sticky note to use it.
- Add text to sticky note and move it to the canvas.
- You can add photos, videos, and files as well as notes.

To share:

- Click on My Page.
- Create groups.
- Invite collaborators.

Finding Images

Many images on the Internet are free to use in your projects. Some require attribution, and some have other limitations. It is important to check the licensing on each image to be sure that you have permission to use the image. If no information is found on the web page, assume that you need to request permission.

American Memory Project from the Library of Congress
http://www.loc.gov/collections
The American Memory Project is an Internet-based archive of public domain image resources from the Library of Congress, as well as audio, video, and archived web content. It is published and updated by the Library of Congress.

AP Images
http://www.apimages.com/Royalty-Free-Images
AP Images includes millions of royalty-free stock photos. Themes include landscape, travel, family, cars, seasons, food, children, pets, and much more available for use from the Associated Press.

British Library
http://www.flickr.com/photos/britishlibrary
The British Library's collections on Flickr Commons offer access to millions of public domain images for you to explore and reuse. There are more than a million images to choose from, and more are being added all the time.

Creative Commons
http://ccsearch.creativecommons.org
CC Search collects data from publicly available sites with open content. CC does not own the images. It is a search engine that searches other sites

that include public domain images and those listed under CC license. Don't assume that the images are under a CC license. You should always follow the link to verify that the work is actually under a CC license and to verify the requirements of that license, including the proper form of attribution.

Digital Public Library of America
http://dp.la
The Digital Public Library of America has shared more than 29 million images, text, and sounds from across the United States.

Every Stock Photo
http://www.everystockphoto.com
This is a search engine for free photos. These come from many sources and are license-specific. You can view a photo's license by clicking on the license icon, below and left of photos. There is not a guarantee that the photo is free to use.

Flickr Advanced Search
http://www.flickr.com/search/advanced/?
You can search through Flickr for images to use. You can limit your search to those photos that are licensed through Creative Commons license.

Free Digital Photos
http://www.freedigitalphotos.net
Download free and premium stock photos and illustrations for use. All of these free images are of high quality. Although free to use in your works, some of the photos come with a small charge for use.

Free Public Domain/CCO Images
http://free-images.com
The site contains millions of free stock photos, art, and vector images. The images are in the public domain or covered under CCO and are free to download and use.

Getty Open Content Program
http://www.getty.edu/about/whatwedo/opencontent.html
The Getty Open Content Program makes all available images in the collection free to use without charge. No permission is required.

Google Images
http://images.google.com
If you use Google, you should do an advanced image search and under usage rights click Labeled for Reuse filter for Free to Use or Share.

Library Artstor
http://library.artstor.org/#/
Core Collections includes access to about 2.5 million images from museums, photo archives, scholars, and artists, and more.

LIFE Photo Archive
http://images.google.com/hosted/life
Search millions of photos from the LIFE photo archive. *Life* magazine was famous for their amazing photos stretching from the 1750s to today. Most of these were never published and are now available for the first time through the joint work of LIFE and Google.

Metropolitan Museum of Art
http://www.metmuseum.org/art/collection
Enjoy searching more than 375,000 images of public domain works from the collection, all of which can be downloaded, shared, and remixed without restriction.

Morguefile
http://morguefile.com
Search the free images. There are more than 350,000 free stock photos that can be used in commercial projects.

National Gallery of Art
http://images.nga.gov/en/page/show_home_page.html
NGA Images is a storehouse of digital images from the collections of the National Gallery of Art. You can search, browse, share, and download images. There are more than 51,000 open access digital images available free of charge.

New York Public Library Digital Collections
http://digitalcollections.nypl.org/search/index
A collection of digital images from the New York Public Library Digital Collections. There are approximately 750,000 images in the database.

Open Photo
http://openphoto.net
The Open Photo Project is a photo-sharing project created in 1998 by Michael Jastremski. Members have offered their images free of charge under terms of Creative Commons licensing.

Pexels
http://www.pexels.com
All photos on Pexels can be used for free for commercial and noncommercial use. Attribution is not required. You can modify the photos.

Photos for Class
http://www.photosforclass.com
The site includes properly attributed, Creative Commons photos for school!

Pics4Learning
http://pics4learning.com
Pics4Learning is a collection of images that are safe and free to use in education. Teachers and students are welcome to use the images for school projects, including websites, videos, or any project in an educational setting.

PIRA Photo Gallery
http://pirc-photogallery.com
This website is filled with copyright free photos to use for noncommercial projects. The photos are contributed by members and organized by category.

Pixabay
http://www.pixabay.com
Pixabay is a community-built site that offers a place to share copyright-free images. Images are covered by Creative Commons CC0 license.

Pixnio Public Domain Images
http://pixnio.com
Pixnio is filled with high-quality images that are free to use. They are not copyrighted. They are public domain images that can be used for personal or commercial use.

Photo Bucket
http://photobucket.com
Photobucket contains thousands of images to use. Content owners can store, edit, and share their images.

PhotoPin
http://photopin.com
This is a search engine that allows you to search millions of Creative Commons photos to use.

Pxhere
http://pxhere.com
Pxhere is a photo-sharing site that offers free copyright images to use for your projects.

StockSnap
http://stocksnap.io
This site has hundreds of images added weekly. They are free from copyright restrictions.

Stock Vault
http://www.stockvault.net
This is a free photo-sharing community. Members can share their work with others all over the world.

Unsplash
http://unsplash.com
Free photos shared by a community of photographers.

Yale Center for British Art
http://britishart.yale.edu
The Yale Center for British Art is a public art museum and research institute. It includes the largest collection of British art outside the United Kingdom.

Wikimedia Commons
http://commons.wikimedia.org/wiki/Main_Page
A collection of 50,202,553 freely usable media files to which anyone can contribute.

Clip Art Resources

There are many times we would like to use clip art in our book promotions. Clip art is useful in illustrating newsletters and other print materials. But clip art is also useful in web pages and social media posts.

- These can be embedded into web pages or social media.
- They make great displays for the library or classroom.
- Use them in animated videos or photos.
- Use them in contests and book quizzes.
- Use them in memes.

Some web pages that are available on the Internet are:

Free ClipArt
http://www.clker.com
Free clip art to use for whatever you need.

Free Clip Art and Images
http://www.incredibleart.org/links/clipart.html
This is a comprehensive list of free clip art that is available for use.

i2Clipart
http://www.i2clipart.com
Royalty-free public domain clip art. Add the Chrome extension to your browser to instantly grab the clip art you need.

Openclipart
http://openclipart.org
This site contains thousands of ready-to-use pieces clip art.

Pixabay
http://pixabay.com/en/photos/clip%20art
Pixabay is an image- and video-sharing community. All contents added to the site are released under Creative Commons CC0 license.

Public Domain Vectors
http://publicdomainvectors.org
This site includes more than 50,000 vector images in the public domain.

Royalty Free Clipart
http://openclipart.org/royalty-free-clipart
This site includes images that can be used many times. There are no restrictions.

Shutterstock Clip Art
http://www.shutterstock.com
Shutterstock has more than 2 million images to use royalty-free. They do charge a small fee for the use of their photos.

WPCLIPART
http://www.wpclipart.com/browse.html
A collection of public domain images. The images are geared to school-age children and should be safe for them to use.

The use of visuals in the reading promotion program scans the gamut from photos aimed at one child to mass marketing aimed at many children. A small postcard picture sent to one child may make a big difference to that child and create a reader.

Visuals are versatile in how they can be employed in your reading promotion program. You can use visuals in print form in large and small formats. Visuals can also be added to social media to reach many more people. And visuals can be combined with videos to create a whole new promotion.

Experiment with different uses of visuals. Using free apps allows you to try new things without a large investment. When you find something that works, the rewards will be great.

CHAPTER TWO

Videos

Talking Avatars

Using talking avatars on a web page or a kiosk is a sure way to attract readers. A talking avatar can be a cartoon character or even a picture that is made to represent a reader's adviser. There are many uses for talking avatars in book promotion. The talking avatar can represent your library in a fun way. And since you can use your own voice to make the avatar speak, you are extending your reach as well as your program's influence.

Here are some ideas for using talking avatars:

- Create a talking avatar to talk about the works of an author. Depending on the avatar used, several books by one author can be promoted. Perhaps the avatar can introduce the first book in a series and mention that there are more.
- The talking avatar could describe a scene from a book.
- Create a talking avatar that discusses multiple titles in a genre. The avatar can describe a genre and recommend books from that genre.
- Use talking avatars to promote library events such as author visits or book clubs.
- Use talking avatars to promote reading challenges.
- Create a talking avatar that introduces students to the state book award nominees to entice them to read them.
- Talking avatars are a good way to promote thematic books or new books.
- Using a digital picture frame or a TV, have your talking avatar greet readers and offer book suggestions as they enter the library or classroom.
- Choose a character on a book cover to promote the book.

- Use your school mascot as your talking avatar.
- Use your avatar in customer service. You can use your voice to deliver your message.

Before creating a talking avatar, determine your overall purpose and what you wish to accomplish. Do you want to emphasize a program, a book, general reading promotion, or other ideas? Do you want to use one talking avatar for all book promotions? Or, would it be better to create several different talking avatars to add diversity?

When you're ready to get started, you'll find there are many good talking avatar creation sites that are available that can help you create an interesting talking avatar. Here are some of the better ones.

Voki
http://www.voki.com

Voki is probably the most popular of the talking avatar creators. The accounts are free, although some characters and props require a paid account. You will need to create a free account to save the talking avatar. The Basic Account is limited. If you upgrade to the paid account, you will get more characters and options. You will also be able to access Voki Presenter. Voki Classroom, a paid service, allows you to create accounts for students to use in a class. Voki is also available as an iOS app and Android app.

Steps to create a Voki talking avatar follow:

- Log in.
- Select an avatar (note: limited characters are available with the Basic Account). You can change the avatar if you decide you don't like it later. There are several categories of avatars, including animals, famous people, holiday symbols, and monsters.
- Once you choose an avatar, customize the avatar. You can choose a hair style, facial characteristics, an outfit, and accessories.
- You can then add a voice. You can add up to 60 seconds of audio. There are multiple ways to add audio.
  - You can record your own voice.
  - You can choose to type your message into a text box and choose a voice to read it. The voices have a variety of accents to choose from.
  - You can upload an audio file to use.
  - If needed, you can actually phone in your message. Voki supplies the phone number and a passcode to use.

- Pick a background from those in the Voki library. There are many backgrounds to choose from in all different themes. Some of the items in Voki are only available in the free account.
- Name your Voki.
- Publish your Voki.
- You can send your talking avatar to social media, send it to your e-mail, or save it to your files. Voki supplies an embed code so you can add it to your web page.

ChatterPix by Duck Duck Moose

Available on iOS only.

ChatterPix is free to use. Rather than creating a cartoon avatar from the app, you can upload a photo to use. The photo should have a mouth showing so that you can designate the area that should move with the audio.

Steps to create a talking avatar follow:

- To begin creating your avatar, you can take a photo or open one from your camera roll.
- You want to be sure that the mouth is showing, so you can make it move.
- Using the app, draw a line where the mouth will open. If you don't get it the way you want it the first time, simply try again.
- You can then record your audio. The limit to 30 seconds. The mouth will move with your audio.
- If you want, you can decorate your picture with added items in the app.
- You can then share via e-mail, save to the camera roll, or upload to YouTube.

PuppetMaster by Shmonster

iPad and iPhone apps.

This free app brings to life any image just by acting it out in front of the iPad or iPhone camera. You can also animate your puppet by touch screen. Book promotions created in this app appeal to younger children as well as teens. You could even have the children create their own book review using a drawing of themselves. (See Figure 2.1)

- There is no login or sign-up required.
- Snap a photo of a drawing or photo to use as your puppet. You can also use one of the ones included in PuppetMaster.

Figure 2.1　PuppetMaster

- Choose a background from the app or take a photo to use your own.
- Animate the avatar by moving and talking in front of the camera. The app picks up the motion, and the puppet moves as you do. Record your audio at the same time. If you do not want to use the motion sensor or can't, you can also animate your character using the touch screen. Record while you are moving your puppet.
- When satisfied, click to save to the camera roll.

Tellagami
tellagami.com

Free iOS app.

Tellagami is a free app that is easy to use and perfect for talking about books as you can have the character talk briefly and describe a book.

Steps for creating an avatar follow:

- Open the app and choose a character. There are several to choose from.
- You can choose your character's emotions so it can be happy, sad, angry, etc.
- Choose a background from those included or upload your own. For book promotion, consider uploading a cover of the book your character is recommending.
- Add text and choose a voice for your character. You can use your own voice and record your text if you wish. You may need to spell unusual words phonetically if you want the character to say them correctly.
- Save the finished project to your camera roll for use on your web page or on social media.

My Talking Avatar

iOS app.

This free app gives you 60 seconds of talk time. The choices of avatar are more limited than for Voki and Chatterpix.

To create your avatar:

- Click on the avatar from the collection included.
- Click to determine whether your character will be male or female.
- Choose the skin color.
- Choose the eye color.
- Choose the mouth.
- Choose the hair style.
- Choose the body type.
- Choose the clothing and accessories.
- Once you have completed your avatar look, you can choose a pose you want. Your avatar can be clapping, laughing, sad, waving, and more. You can even add an additional character to your avatar. There are additional poses included in the paid account.
- When you are happy with your avatar, click the check mark to continue.
- You can add text to your avatar. There is a limited ability to change font.
- You can record your message and click the check mark when you are done.
- You can go back to change any of the items if you choose. When satisfied, save to the camera roll.

Blabberize
http://www.blabberize.com

This is a free web-based talking avatar site. You need to be running Flash to use Blabberize.

To create your avatar:

- Click on Make.
- Find a picture and upload the file.
- You will be prompted to crop the picture to use just the area you want to use in the avatar.
- Click Next.
- You will see an orange circle that you will need to drag and use to designate the mouth area. To add a mouth, use the sizing handles to position it and

proportion it. The green circle indicates where the flap of the mouth will be when it is talking. Creating the mouth is the most difficult part of using this site.

- You can then add your sound. You can either record your own voice or upload an audio file you have already recorded. The mouth will move in reaction to the audio.
- If you do not like the way the avatar looks, you can go back and make changes.
- When you are satisfied, save the talking avatar. It will save to the Blabberize site.
- When saved, you can e-mail the Blabber to yourself or others, or you can create an embed code to add the avatar to your social media or web page.

Talking Pets

Talking Pets is an app that allows you to create a talking avatar. You can add your pet or any animal to speak for you. You do not need to log in or create an account to use the app.

To use Talking Pets:

- Open the app.
- Select the photo you want to use from your camera roll, or take a picture with your camera to use.
- Adjust the photo size and orientation to fit in the box provided.
- When happy with the way your photo fits, click Choose.
- Using the on-screen markers, adjust to position chin, mouth, and eyes.
- Click Next.
- Click Record button to start your recording. Record your voice to say what you want to say.
- Click Record button again to stop recording.
- Your video preview will appear.
- The voice on the video will not be your voice but one created by the app.
- You can add filters by swiping the image.
- When finished, share to social media, e-mail, or save to camera roll.

Talking Pets avatars can be used on your social media or web pages to promote books. You can even use an animal to promote animal books! Have a talking pig promote books that have a pig theme. If you have a

"Read to the Dogs" event, have the dog promote it and some book suggestions.

Animate Me

Animate Me is an app that can be used to create a talking avatar. There is no need to create an account and sign in. It is available in iOS and Android.

To use Animate Me:

- Open the app.
- Click on the picture to start.
- Choose a photo to use as the background photo. The background picture will hold the talking avatar. Choose from album (camera roll), camera, or Facebook.
- Move and scale the image. You can flip from side to side or up and down.
- Click Add Face.
- Choose a face to animate.
- Zoom in on the face.
- Adjust mouth lines.
- Add props.
- To record sound, click on Record button.
- Save sound.
- Preview video.

To save the video, you will need the pro account. If you have access to a screen recorder on the device, you can use that. If you plan to use this app more than once, it is suggested that you purchase a pro account for $4.99.

Morpho

Morpho allows you to use a photo and morph it into a new character. There is a limited free version and a paid premium version that allows for more effects. The free version allows you to create characters that can be morphed.

To use Morpho:

- Create a free account using your e-mail address.
- Open app.

- Click Create.
- Choose a photo from your camera roll or take a photo. Click Done.
- Touch, pinch, and zoom to frame the head within the template. Click Done.
- Touch, pinch, and zoom to frame the left eye within the template. Click Done.
- Touch, pinch, and zoom to frame the right eye within the template. Click Done.
- Touch, pinch, and zoom to frame the nose within the template. Click Done.
- Touch, pinch, and zoom to frame the mouth within the template. Click Done.
- Finish or go back to edit the elements again.
- If you are using the free app, click Cancel for costumes.
- Record your message.
- You can change the pitch of your voice.
- Preview.
- You will need the paid account to share through the app.

To save the video on an iOS device:

- Go to Settings.
- Go to Control Center.
- Go to Customize Controls.
- Click on Camera to include in the Control Center.
- Go back to Morph video.
- Swipe up from the bottom to bring up the Control Center.
- Click the camera Record button.
- Drop the Control Center screen and play the Morph video.
- When finished, bring up the Control Center and stop recording.
- Your video will be saved in your camera roll.
- Edit the video to trim any unneeded parts.
- Save.

Video Editors

Videos are a great way to grab the attention of children as they love watching videos. Videos can be used in a variety of ways to promote reading. They can be embedded into web pages or shown on screens in the library.

Here are some ideas for using videos in book promotion:

- Use videos to promote library events such as author visits, book clubs, or book parties.
- Use videos to promote reading challenges like the number of books read by different classes.
- Use a character to promote a book. The character can give a book talk for the book.
- Create a video of an author's work. The video could show a scene from a book.
- Create a video that stresses titles in a genre. Characters can discuss a genre and recommend books from that genre.
- Create a video of the state book award nominees to entice students to read them.
- Videos are a good way to promote thematic books or new books.

Before beginning to create any visuals, determine your purpose. Do you want to emphasize a program, a book, general reading promotion, or other ideas? Once you have determined your purpose, begin to construct a storyboard. Rough out how you want the video to look. Then prepare a script. It is much easier to record the audio for the video with a prepared script. A script will help you determine what the characters will look like or what they will be doing. You can then create your video. If you are going to use photos in your video, decide which ones and have them ready.

Many good video makers are available that can help you create an interesting video that will be enjoyed by your patrons. In addition to MovieMaker for PC and iMovie for Mac, there are many free apps that make it easy to create videos for book promotion.

Adobe Spark Video
http://spark.adobe.com

Adobe Spark Video can be used in your web browser. It is also available as an iOS app. Sign up for a free account with your Google account or Facebook account, or create an account using your e-mail. (See Figure 2.2)

Steps for creating the video follow:

- Log in to the app.
- Click on the plus sign and choose Video.
- You can use a template or start your video from scratch.

Figure 2.2   Adobe Spark Video

- Add a title (what's your story about?).
- Click Next.
- Choose layout, theme, and music. You do not need to use music.
- Once in the slide, you can insert text, video, photos, or icons.
- To insert video, upload from camera roll or file.
- Photos can be loaded from camera roll, Dropbox, or social media, or you can take a photo while in Spark.
- To record, hold orange microphone icon and record your audio.
- Click on plus sign on bottom left to add each new slide.
- When you are finished, click Share.
- This will create a link.
- Note: you can also download the movie to your device.

Quik by GoPro
http://gopro.com

Quik is a free, easy-to-use app for iOS and Android as well as a download. (See Figure 2.3)
To use the mobile app:

- Select photos and videos from your camera roll.
- Choose the video style from the available styles.
- You can then edit your video.
  - Add photos.
  - Add text slides.

Figure 2.3 Quik by GoPro

- You can edit your text slides.
    - You can delete slides or text if desired.
    - Then choose duration that the slides will show.
    - You can also duplicate slides.
- Edit photos:
    - Add text overlays.
    - Delete photos.
    - Adjust rotation, zoom in, flip.
    - Choose point of focus.
    - Choose duration of slide.
    - Fit to screen.
    - Duplicate photos.
- Edit video clips:
    - Add text overlays.
    - Delete clips.
    - Add, edit, or remove highlights.
    - Trim.
    - Adjust rotation.
    - Add sound.
    - Adjust speed.
    - Fit to screen.
    - Duplicate clips.
- Choose music to use in your video. Music can be uploaded or chosen from the built-in music.
- Organize the video.
- Choose video options:
    - Duration.
    - Format—cinema, square, portrait.
    - Music start point.
- Save and share. You can share on social media, download to computer, or save to your camera roll.

WeVideo
https://www.wevideo.com/

WeVideo is available for download on the web. It is also available on mobile devices. The free Basic Account is limited to one 5-minute video

Figure 2.4 WeVideo

per month, 1-GB storage, 22 songs, and download to local device. (See Figure 2.4)

To create a video using the iPad app:

- Click Create.
- Choose photos and/or videos from your camera roll.
- Hold and drag the images to the timeline.
- Click on the icon between slides to choose transitions.
- Choose a theme.
- Click Done.
- You can keep the music that is included with the theme or choose from the media library.
- Choose the microphone icon if you wish to add audio overlay.
- To change the duration of photo slide, click the slide, click on duration, and change the timing.
- Click Done.
- To change the title of the movie:
    - Click the title slide.

- Edit the title.
- Click Done.
- You can also turn the slides, rotate the pictures, flip the slide, or blur the background.
- Save the video to the camera roll to use with your projects.

Typito
http://www.typito.com

Typito is free but shows branding on the free videos. The branding is not intrusive; nor does it block the video. It simply shows the Typito logo. The free Basic Account is limited to four videos. Typito is a desktop app only.

To create a video:

- You must create a login to use Typito.
- Sign in to your account.
- Create a video by clicking on the plus sign.
- Upload your video image.
- By default, Typito will play for 20 seconds. You can change the time by scrolling on the marker icon under the photo.
- Add text by clicking the text icon on the left.
  - Choose location, font, color, and effects using the tools.
  - Type the text.
- To add images, click on the media icon and add another image.
  - Add at end.
  - Choose time duration.
  - Add text.
- You can add audio by uploading your own or choosing from the built-in library.
- Edit as needed.
- Click on Export and choose Yes.
- You can download the video or send it to social media.

Clips Video

Clips is a free iOS app. Use Clips for quick videos that can be put on web pages or social media. Clips is very easy to use and creates small files that are great for web pages and social media. (See Figure 2.5)

- Open the app.
- To create a new video, click on the file folder icon in the upper left.
- Click the plus sign to create a new video.
- Click the camera icon. Choose front-facing or rear-facing camera.
- Take photos or record video.
- Add photos from your camera roll if wanted.
- Add filters, labels, stickers, or emojis by clicking the star icon.
- Add a title slide by clicking on posters.

Figure 2.5   Clips

- You can record live titles—speak while recording to add text.
- Add soundtracks from built-in library or use your own.
- Save video to camera roll, social media, or e-mail.
- Clips only works with iOS.

Biteable
http://biteable.com

Biteable makes videos in a snap. Biteable is a desktop app that is easy to use; it's great for making on-the-spot videos. You can create an account using your Google account, Facebook account, or your e-mail.

To create a video:

- Click on Make Video.
- You can skip the question "I'm making a video for . . ."
- Use "I'm making a video to . . ."
- Look through the templates provide or Start from Scratch.
- Add a title.
- Click Get Started.
- Pick a scene.
- You can upload your own photos.
- Add animation.

- Add footage.
- Add content—add text (you can change the font).
- Add scene for additional scenes.
- When you have added all the scenes you want, click Preview. It may take a few minutes for the video to compile.
- Go back to edit or click Publish when done.
- You will get an embed code and a video link.
- You will need the premium account to download the video.

Biteable is a good application to use to create book trailers. It is quick and easy and creates interesting videos.

Videoshop

Videoshop is an iOS and Android app with a quick video creation and editing tool. Using Videoshop, you can add music, sound effects, subtitles, and other effects to your video. You can easily share your videos on social media.

Here's how you use Videoshop:

- There is no need to sign in or create an account.
- Open app.
- Record video or import video from camera roll.
- Click on Edit.
  - Add text and adjust font, color, and text effects.
  - Place text on video timeline to determine where the text will go.
  - Add voice by clicking on the voice button.
  - Place voice on video timeline to determine where the voice will go.
  - Add sounds by clicking the Sounds button. Sounds include music from your library or sounds from the app.
  - Place sounds on video timeline to determine where the sound will go.
  - Add tracks by clicking on Sounds and choosing Tracks. Tracks differ from sounds. Sounds are short bursts of sound. Tracks will play for a longer duration.
  - Place tracks on video timeline to determine where the track will go. The track can play through the entire video.
  - If desired, add another video clip by clicking on the plus sign.

- Press Next.
- Once compiled, you can change filters and add a theme.
- Add a title, author, location, and date.
- Save the video to your camera roll or social networking site.

Videoshop is a quick video creator that allows you to create videos on the go. Videos can be used to show new books, genres, book talks by staff, or even create book trailers to add to your social networks or web page.

Koma Koma

Koma Koma is an iOS app. Koma Koma is an easy-to-use, stop-motion video app. There is no need to sign in or create an account.

To use Koma Koma:

- Open app.
- Click on the wrench icon to bring up settings.
- Determine frames per second for the video. The more frames per second, the faster the pictures will appear.
- You can reverse the photos left to right, up and down, and add fading.
- Choose Onion Skin to show where your photo is in relation to the next one taken. This makes the stop-motion effect easier.
- Time lapse allows you to set up your app to take photos over a length of time. You can set the time interval between photos for your video. You can choose up to 10 minutes between shots.
- You can slow down and speed up the video after it is completed if you do not like how it looks.
- To delete a photo, click on the blue X. This will delete one photo.
- To save your project to the gallery, click on the yellow button.
- You can then play the video, add a title, edit, save to the camera roll, or delete the video.
- The button on the top right brings up the gallery.

Stop-motion video can be used to showcase a group of books. Each shot can be a different book cover. The speed can be set to be sure the covers can be seen by the viewers. A slow-motion video can be added to your social media sites or to your web page. The video can be used as a book carousel on your site.

Funimate

Funimate is an app similar to Clips but can be used on an Android device.

Green Screen Apps

Using a green screen app in video production opens up the world to your book promotion activities. Green screens allow you to make your real-life backgrounds disappear and be replaced by images of other places. Use travel backgrounds or fantasy worlds to give more pizazz to your photos or videos. The app lets you erase the real-life background or anything with that color. Be careful with what you wear in from of a green screen as you may end up "losing" part of your body.

Here's how you set up the green screen background:

- A professional green screen is the best to use but not the only alternative.
- Use green table cloth. Be sure there are no wrinkles in the cloth, which may interfere with the green screen effect.
- Use green bulletin board paper.
- Use a wrinkle-free green bed sheet.
- Use wrinkle-free green fabric tacked to the wall.

If you are using something other than a professional green screen, be sure the shade of your alternative is close to the green of a green screen on the app. (See Figure 2.6, Figure 2.7)

Before beginning any video project, you should storyboard your project. This will help when you are filming your project. Having rough drawings of the different scenes will help when you begin to video. For video, it is good to have a script prepared as well. Some video programs use teleprompters built into the app, and it is helpful to have a written script to follow.

Figure 2.6   Green Screen

Figure 2.7   Green Screen

Green Screen by Do Ink
www.doink.com

This is one of the most popular green screen apps used in education. It is easy to use and creates great green screen videos.

To use Green Screen by Do Ink:

- Record your video in front of the green screen. You can use the iPad camera app. If needed, create all video clips that will make up your video.
- Be sure none of your actors are wearing the same color as the green screen as the app will make anything that color disappear.
- Choose a background photo for video from your camera roll. Import the photo of video into your camera roll if you are using an outside source.
- In the app, you will see three timeline layers on the bottom of the screen.
- On the bottom timeline, add your background photo or video.
- The video you have created will be placed on the middle timeline.

- The top timeline can be used for adding animation to the video.
- Save to camera roll, social media, and/or e-mail.

TouchCast Studio
www.touchcast.com/studio

TouchCast Studio is a free iPad app that allows you to make videos using templates. Use the green screen effect to put yourself in a newsroom, in front of the Lincoln Memorial, and many more. If you do not want to use one of the green screen backgrounds, you can add your own.

- You need to create a free account. You can sign in with your Google account or your Facebook account, or create an account with your e-mail address.
- Choose your background from those included in the app. The ready-made backgrounds include newsroom, annotate a web page, annotate a video, annotate an image, map, file, livestream, talk show set, Lincoln Memorial, newscast, business, sports, Here's How, live stream, and Review It. If you are reviewing a book for your book promotion program, you might want to use the Review It template.
- Gather all the elements you will use for your video. Called Vapps, you can include photos, maps, images, videos, files, Google maps, Twitter streams, and many more.
- As you prepare your production, add all Vapps in the order you will use them, upload your script into the teleprompter, and add other features you plan to use in the production.
- To start your video, click on New TouchCast. You will also see My Projects and My TouchCasts. Projects are those that you may have already worked on but did not finalize. My TouchCasts are where you will find your completed projects.
- In postproduction mode, you can edit scenes by touching the segment and selecting Trim.
- Save:
  - To TouchCast Fabric.
  - To publish on YouTube.
  - To save to your camera roll.
- TouchCast Project is not yet finalized. All Vapps and teleprompter are ready.
- TouchCast video ready to save and play.

Green Screen Pro

Only available for Mac iOS.

* Open Green Screen Pro.
* Select color of green screen. This color will be removed and replaced by the background image.
* In the camera viewer, adjust the slider until it looks good.
* Record your video.
* Save to your camera roll or share with social media.

Animated Videos

Animated videos are a great way to grab the attention of children. They are colorful and often fast-paced and eye-catching. Animated videos can be used in a variety of ways to promote reading.

* They can be embedded into web pages or shown on screens in the library.
* Use animated videos to promote library events such as author visits and book clubs.
* Use animated videos to promote reading challenges such as number of pages read, number of books read, etc.
* Use a character to promote a book. The character can give a book talk for the book.
* Create an animated video of an author's work. The video could show a scene from a book.
* Create an animated video that stresses titles in a genre. Characters can discuss a genre and recommend books from that genre.
* Create an animated video of the state book award nominees to entice students to read them.
* Animated videos are a good way to promote thematic books or new books. Use a video to highlights books on a specific theme such as holidays, historical time periods, community events, etc.

Before beginning to create any visual, determine your purpose. Do you want to emphasize a program, a book, general reading promotion, or other ideas? Once you have determined your purpose, begin constructing your storyboard. Rough out how you want the video to look. Then prepare a script. It is much easier to record the audio for the video with a prepared script. A script will help you determine what the characters will look like or what they will be doing. Will they be human or animal or other? You can then create your animated video.

There are many good animated video makers that are available that can help you create an interesting video that will be enjoyed by your patrons.

Sock Puppets by SmithMicro

Sock Puppets is a free app available for iPads and iPhones. You do not need to sign up or create an account to use the app. You can make a video of up to 30 seconds. An upgraded paid account allows longer videos.

Steps to creating the video follow:

- Download the app from the App Store.
- Open the app and look around to see what features are available.
- Choose NEW to create a new video.
- On the Character Select Screen, choose one or more sock puppet characters to be in your movie.
- On the Background Select Screen, choose a background for your story.
- On the Props and Scenery Screen, choose which items, if any, to add to your movie. Items framed in yellow will move. Those in red will not.
- You can go back and edit any items that you wish.
- To record audio, tap on the sock puppet that you wish to speak. Tap the red record button and speak. If you have more than one sock puppet, you can get each to speak by tapping on it. Your voice will be converted into sock speak. Each sock puppet will have a different voice.
- The video is limited to 30 seconds in the free mode.
- To save, click on save icon. You can save to the camera roll, iCloud, or YouTube.

Note: Although the videos are limited to 30 seconds, you can make a longer video by saving multiple clips and loading them into movie-editing software, which can stitch them together into a longer video.

Animoto
http://www.animoto.com

There are free educator accounts available, but they must be requested. Animoto is web based and also available for iOS and Android. Unique videos can be created using Animoto. You can use graphics, effects, and transitions on your photos; add sound and you have a simple video. If you don't like how the video looks, you can simply render it again and a new effect is created. The tempo of the music will determine how quickly your photos will transition.

The free videos are limited to 30 seconds, so the book talks will need to be very quick and simple. Longer videos can be created for a cost or in the educator account.

To use Animoto, you need to register. Sign up for a free account. You will need to supply your e-mail address and choose a username and password. Click on the sign-up link to get started, and then fill in the required information.

Now you are all set to create your Animoto video. Be sure to storyboard the video and prepare the script in advance. You need a minimum of 10 images to create an Animoto video. Although you can use a music track, for a book talk you should record your book talk using other software and save it as an MP3 file. Once the images are saved and the audio is recorded, you are ready to make your Animoto video as easy as 1–2–3.

To use Animoto:

- Upload the images for your presentation, and then arrange them in the order you wish them to appear.
- Upload your book talk audio MP3 file by clicking on the Upload button, then browsing and choosing the file. Alternatively, you can use the built-in music.
- Click to finalize your video. It may take a few minutes to render your video, depending on how many pictures you use. You will need to give your presentation a name and a description and also add your name.
- Finally, sit back and enjoy your presentation.

Toontastic
http://toontastic.com

Toontastic is a popular, free animation tool. Students may have used this app and may even be familiar with the characters, so they might feel as if they are getting recommendations from friends. There are both iOS and Android apps. No login is required. (See Figure 2.8)

- Open the app.
- Click on the plus sign to begin.
- Choose story format:
  - Short story (three parts). Short story may be the best option for a book trailer.

Figure 2.8   Toontastic

- • Classic story (five parts).
- • Science report (five parts).
- Click Beginning.
- Pick a setting or draw your own background.
- Add characters or draw your own. You can use the "draw your own" feature to add a book title and author to the video.
- When you have picked out your characters, click on →. Position your character(s) and click Start to record your narration.
- Click red button to stop recording.
- You can add music to your slide. Choose an emotion from the bottom tool bar to add music that matches the mood.
- Click the check mark to accept the slide.
- Continue making more slides for as many as you need.
- Click Finish when you are done.
- You will be prompted to add a title and your name.
- Review your video and edit it where needed.
- When ready, export the video to your camera roll.

Moovly
http://www.moovly.com

Moovly is a free app that is web based and available for iOS and Android. You do need to sign up for an account. To sign up for a free educator account, you need to use a school e-mail address and request the free account. The account allows 1 GB of storage and unlimited downloads in standard definition (SD). (See Figure 2.9)

Figure 2.9 Moovly

- Open the app and be sure you are on the Dashboard. Any previous videos, or moovs, will be on the Dashboard.

- Click on Create Moov.

- You will see the Library on the left. The Library includes thousands of items that can be used in your moov. These include pictures, videos, and sounds. Additionally, you can upload your own.

- In the middle of the screen is the Stage. This is where you will build slides.

- At the bottom you'll find the timeline. This is where you will control the movement in the video. Determine when pictures will appear, when audio starts, etc., by sliding the timeline.

- The Properties box appears on the right. Properties offers you the opportunity to control how the objects move or add text boxes to the Stage.

- To begin:
  - Pick an object from the Library and drag it to the stage.
  - Place, relocate, size, rotate, or edit the object.
  - Some objects have additional properties that you can adjust in the Properties section.

- Add text and control how it appears by using the Properties box.

- Add animation by dragging to the Stage and determining the duration by using the timeline.

- When you are finished, you can upload the video or save to camera roll.

Shadow Puppet Edu

Shadow Puppet Edu is a quick and easy way to take pictures and put them into a video with narration. In addition to your own photos, collections from other sites are available within the app. It is available as an iPad app.

To use the app:

- Open the app.
- Click on Create New.
- You will see a selection page where you can select pictures from your camera roll. You will also be directed to collections of famous landmarks, Library of Congress collection, Metropolitan Museum of Art collection, The British Library Collection, NASA, and NOAA.
- Select the photos you want to use.
- Click Next.
- You will see your first image. You can then zoom the photo.
- Add text (effects, font, color, and size).
- You can choose background music if desired. Preview the included music, and select the one you want.
- Click Start.
- Record your voice if you are using narration.
- If using multiple pictures, swipe left to get to the next photo.
- When finished, click the Record button to stop.
- Preview and save.
- Add title.
- Click Done.
- It is automatically saved to the camera roll.

This is a user-friendly app that makes creating short, narrated videos quick and easy. The inclusion of the photo collection from other sites makes finding good images simple.

Draw and Tell by Duck Duck Moose

Draw and Tell is available as an iOS app and is a fun app to use to create annotated photos or voice-over videos. There is no need to create an account.

To use Draw and Tell:

- Open the app.
- Click Blank Paper.
- To use a photo, click on the Photo Paper.

- Choose a photo from camera roll.
- Photo will appear in the center.
- Use tools along the edges of the screen to enhance the photo.
- Use the crayon, pencil, or paint to write or draw on the photo.
- Erase any mistakes using the eraser tool.
- Add stickers if you wish.
- Once you have annotated the photo, you can add a voice message.
- Click the audio button on the top of the page.
- Lines you draw while recording will not show.
- Stickers that are moved while recording will show on final video.
- When finished recording, click up arrow to save.
- If you want to create a longer video, stack several videos and then save them.
- Select drawing to save to camera roll.
- Save to photos.

Draw and Tell is an easy app to use. You can even have some of your students help with book promotion by creating videos to share.

Sharalike Slideshow

Available for iOS and Android.

Sharalike Slideshow is an application that allows users to quickly organize and create video slideshows. Automatically sort and enhance your pictures and videos to create a video slideshow. You will need to create an account to save the slideshow.

To create the slideshow:

- Open the app.
- Click on Get Started.
- Sign in or create an account. You can use your e-mail address or Facebook.
- Click New.
- Select photos.
- Click the check mark in the upper right when all desired photos are selected.
- You will be able to:
  - Rearrange the photos.
  - Change the theme of the slideshow.

- Add music.
- Change the photos selected or add additional ones.
- Change the introduction and/or credits.
- When the smartshow is finished, save to social media or e-mail it.

You will be able to mark the slideshow as private if you do not want it available on the Internet.

Sharalike is a good app for making quick videos to share on your web page or social media. You can add videos of book events or quick book slideshows.

Augmented Reality

Augmented reality is a technology that superimposes computer-generated images onto a user's view of the real world, providing an augmented view of the world. Augmented reality provides users with an interactive experience that changes the way they look at the world. The popularity of augmented reality reached millions when Pokémon Go took off in 2016. In the game, players used a smartphone and app to discover characters from the game. Those without the app could not see the character.

Augmented reality is becoming more popular in education as well as in marketing. IKEA allows users to find out additional information about items simply by launching an app and pointing a smartphone at the object.

Augmented reality has also proven very useful in education—from individualized education to group work and beyond. When used with reading and book promotion, augmented reality puts the children in control of what they see and read.

More and more books are being published using augmented features to entertain and to teach. It is a natural extension of reading to augment with added information or even video. Since 2014, *Guinness World Book of Records* has included augmented photos in the book. Used along with their app, readers can view videos of the world records.

Here's a selected list of books being published with augmented photos:

Bradley, C. Grimm. *Goodnight Lad*. Hidden Worlds, 2016.
This book uses augmented reality to bring the book to life. Each page contains augmented animations that kids love to play with.

Bridges, Shirin Yim. *Horrible: An Augmented Collection of Ghosts and Ghouls*. Goosebottom Books, 2012.

This is a ghost book with a twist. Or should I say augmented material? There are 10 famous tales of ghost stories through time. The use of augmentation allows the ghost stories to come to life.

Ganeri, Anita. *iStorm: Wild Weather and Other Forces of Nature.* **Carlton Kids, Carlton Books Limited, 2014.**
Includes text and photographs that explore various forces of nature, including blizzards, tornados, earthquakes, wildfires, and droughts.

Harrington, Kim. *Close Encounters of the Nerd Kind.* **Sterling Children's Books, 2017.**
When Bex and Charlie try Veratrum Games Corp's new augmented reality game, featuring aliens instead of monsters, they attract two aliens, kind Vera and evil Bob, to Earth.

iDinosaur. **Carlton Books, 2013.**
Provides descriptions of the various kinds of dinosaurs that lived millions of years ago in a book that includes an application that allows the reader to experience augmented reality animations of some of the dinosaurs.

McLeod, Patrick. *An Elephant in Our Garden.* **Createspace, 2013.**
Something is eating all the vegetables in Daddy's garden. Isabella thinks it might be an elephant or a bear or even a penguin. Follow along in this who-done-it mystery of vegetable carnage. The cover and four interior pages of this book have been infused with augmented reality. Bring them to life with your iOS or Android device that contains a front-facing camera. Requires an Internet connection.

Steele, Michael Anthony. *Attack of the Zombie Mermaids: A 4d Book.* **Picture Window Books, 2019.**
While searching for undersea treasure, Captain Banana Beard and the Nearly Fearless Monkey Pirates find Neptune's Trident, which is cursed, and are immediately attacked by zombie mermaids.

Steele, Michael Anthony. *Battle of the Pirate Bands: A 4d Book.* **Picture Window Books, 2019.**
It is time for the greatest of pirate competitions, to see which pirate band is the best; but when the prize trophy is stolen, the other bands are quick to blame the Monkey Pirates—and only Mr. Pickles, the youngest monkey, can save them from walking the plank.

Steele, Michael Anthony. *Escape from Haunted Treasure Island: A 4d Book.* **Picture Window Books, 2019.**
When the Nearly Fearless Monkey Pirates land on an island in search of treasure, they find themselves surrounded by monkey pirate ghosts who are determined to protect it—and only Mr. Pickles, the youngest of Captain Banana Beard's crew, can save them from being dropped into a volcano.

Steele, Michael Anthony. *Hunt for the Octo-Shark: A 4d Book.* **Picture Window Books, 2019.**
When his crew expresses doubts about the existence of the octo-shark, a creature that is half octopus and half shark, Captain Banana Beard of the Nearly Fearless Monkey Pirates and his crew set out on a hunt to find the mythical monster—but the search nearly turns all of them into an octo-shark lunch.

Nonfiction books work very well with augmented reading. The majority of augmented books being published are nonfiction. Capstone Publishing has several series of books that are published with augmented content. The series include country books, animal books, STEM-themed books, human anatomy books, and others. These all come with content that can be accessed with an app. Other publishers are working on using augmented reality with nonfiction books. Popar also publishes a line of augmented books.

In addition to the many sources of augmented content that is available from commercial sources, it is possible to use apps to create your own augmented experiences. There are many uses for augmented reality in education. In book promotion, it is a natural to use this technology to entice children to read.

Uses for augmented reality for book promotion follow:

- Books seem to come to life even on the shelves when that have an aura attached to them. Students can use their devices to hear a book talk or watch a video of the author reading from the book.
- Pictures of authors can come to life when an aura is attached. The authors can introduce you to their books or simply offer a message about the importance of reading.
- Genres can be discussed when an aura is attached to a picture.
- Librarians, teachers, and children can give their take on a book when an aura is attached to the cover.

HP Reveal (formerly Aurasma)
http://studio.hpreveal.com

HP Reveal is a free app that is available as a web-based app as well as for iOS and Android devices. To create an account, you will need to sign up using your e-mail address and choosing a username.

Before you begin, it is helpful to understand the terminology used by HP Reveal. The trigger and overlay do not have to be saved to the Internet, making HP Reveal ideal for recording children talking about books. If the aura is tagged as Private, only those with permission can view the files.

Trigger: A trigger is an image or object in real life that will activate the augmented experience.

Overlay: An overlay is usually a video that will begin playing when the trigger is viewed. This can be a video that is saved in your files or it can be a YouTube video.

Aura: An aura is the complete experience that includes both the trigger and the overlay.

Once you have signed in to your account, you will be able to see all the auras that you have created as well as public auras that have been created by others.

To create a new aura:

- Name the aura.
- Upload the trigger image from your files, or select from existing photos on Dropbox or Google Drive. To find the image, click on Browse. Name the trigger image. Add a description.
- Upload the overlay and name the file. The video can be found using the Browse function. If you are using a video that is published on the Internet, enter the URL for the video. Name the overlay file and add a description.
- Adjust the size and determine the action taken. The video can fade in or out or other actions.
- Save and preview.
- Click Next and add name and hash tag.
- Save.
- Share. The aura can be either public or private.

Viewing the aura: Children can view the aura on their devices. They must have the HP Reveal app and be logged in to the same account as that used to create the aura. Alternatively, you can publish to a channel and have children follow the channel.

When a device is aimed at the trigger, in this case a book cover, a swirl appears and then the video begins. When the device is moved away, the video will stop playing.

Metaverse
http://studio.gometa.io

Metaverse is a platform that lets anyone create interactive content in augmented reality. Metaverse can be accessed as a web-based program, iOS, and Android. It is a free program that allows use of many augmented experiences as well as the means to create your own.

- The first step is to create an account. You can sign in using your Facebook account, or create an account using your e-mail.
- Once you are signed in, you will be able to see your experiences as well as many others that have been created by other users. You can add comments to the experiences. You can copy experiences and edit them to make them your own.
- To create your own experience, click on Create Experience button.
- This will bring you to the storyboard. One scene is already there for you to edit.
- Add a title for the experience.
- Click on Character Scene and select your character from the library.
- Add dialog to the character.
- Optionally, add music.
- Click on the plus sign to add a new scene.
- To link the scenes, click on Transition to Screen and click on the first scene.
- Optionally, create a frame.
- When you have added all the scenes you want, click on End Experience.
- You can preview your experience. A QR code is generated. Print the QR code or add it to a web page or social media.
- Open the Metaverse app on your device and scan the QR code.
- Your first scene will appear in your environment. If there is more than one scene, a plus sign appears on the screen to go to the next screen.
- When you have finished creating your experience, click Publish.

- Add a description, category, and location.
- Share the QR code with your children so they can participate in the experience.

Metaverse Breakouts

Metaverse maintains a public spreadsheet, which tracks new AR content across subjects and grade levels that are available to use (https://tinyurl.com/y6vpf2az).

Just a Line

Just a Line is an iOS and Android app that allows you to draw on reality and record the image. While viewing reality through the app, simply touch the screen and begin to draw. You can record and share what you have drawn. You do not need to create an account or sign in to use the app.
To use Just a Line:

- Open app.
- Aim camera at what you want to use to write on.
- Choose the size of the line you want by clicking on the circles on the bottom left side of the screen.
- Touch the screen and draw.
- If you want to create a video of your augmented item, click on the Record button.
- You can also draw with a partner.
- You can record just the video, or you can add audio.
- Save to camera roll or share with social media.

Use Just a Line to highlight books you want to share. You can point to the books in the video or even draw stars or circles around the book. Sharing these on social media or web pages is a good way to interest children in books.

Thyng

Thyng is an iOS and Android app that allows you to augment reality using photos, animations, or videos. There are many items included in the app that can be added to reality to create a video. You do not need to create an account or log in to use the app.

To use Thyng:

- Open the app.
- Choose Surfaces and tap to view.
- You will see the buttons along the sides.
- Find a surface to use as your platform. This can be a tabletop, floor, or any flat surface. The app will frame the surface in green when it is ready.
- Add an object from the built-in gallery, or select a photo from your camera roll.
- You can add photos.
- You can add videos.
- To reset the size of the object, use button on the left of the screen to enlarge or decrease the size of the object.
- Rotate object using the buttons on the left.
- The camera icon takes a screen shot.
- To add another object to the scene, click the plus sign.
- When your augmented object is where you want it, you can record your video. You can record just video, or you can record both audio and video.
- Click the Record button to begin your recording. Click again to stop.
- Your Thyng is saved to your camera roll.

Using Thyng allows you to easily create short, augmented videos to use in book promotion. Try using a book cover as your surface and having an object talking about the book on top of it. These short videos can be used on your social media sites or on web pages.

Virtual Reality

The technology of virtual reality (VR) allows students to submerge themselves into an entirely new reality. The reader uses a headset to block out reality, so the virtual world is the only thing they see. VR is growing fast in popularity, and more and more virtual worlds are being created. It is now even possible to create your own VR world to suit your needs.

Children are fascinated with VR and are generally eager to try new experiences. However, some children find that the experience may lead to motion sickness or headaches. Also, there is caution about using VR with very young children.

VR can be used in a variety of ways to promote reading:

- Use VR to promote library reading events including author visits and book club events.
- Use VR to extend understanding of novels. You can use VR to give a travel tour of the location of the novel.
- Use VR to promote books using summaries embedded into virtual space.

Before beginning to use any VR, determine your purpose. Do you want to emphasize a program, a book, general reading promotion, or other ideas?

There are many good VR tours ready to use on the Internet. You may want to explore some of these before you think about creating your own.

Finding Virtual Reality

Google Expeditions

Google has taken the lead in VR for education. Google Expeditions is a free program that can be used in schools. There are hundreds of Expeditions that can be guided by teachers. Expeditions can be used to extend knowledge of a location so students can picture the setting of a book. For example, students reading *Lord of the Flies* can take a virtual trip to an island in the Pacific Ocean to experience what the characters may have encountered.

Google Street View

Google Street View contains many VR trips that highlight views from around the world. Unlike the Google Expeditions, these trips are suited to individual viewing. You can use a premade VR trip to highlight a collection of books. For example, you can have children take a virtual trip to London to promote books that take place in London.

YouTube

There are many VR trips on YouTube. To search for them:

- Search for what you are looking for, e.g., children's books.
- Click on Filter.
- Use the 360° filter.

- Results should all be 360° videos that meet your search criteria.
- YouTube also has a VR Channel that you can search.

The VR videos can be viewed in VR goggles to give the children the true VR experience.

Creating Your Own Virtual Reality

It is not difficult to create your own VR. There have been many apps created in the past few years that make it easier. Also, new smartphone cameras make it simple to create panoramas to use in VR.

Panoroo
http://www.panoroo.com

Panoroo is a free web-based site. The free account is limited to three tours. You need to create an account to use Panoroo. You can sign in with Facebook or LinkedIn or create an account with e-mail.

Steps to creating a VR tour follow:

- A tour is a collection of scenes that can be stitched together to create a 360° panorama. Each scene is one 360°. Alternatively, you can use a panorama video.
- Click Create Tour.
- Name your tour. The tour should have a name that describes the tour.
- Add a description.
- Click Create.
- Select type of panorama:
    - Upload 360° video.
    - Upload photos to stitch into panorama.
- Upload.
- Click Open.
- Wait for Upload to finish before closing or continuing.
- You should name a scene to let viewers know what they are looking at.
- Click on the Thumbnail to select the scene.
- Click on Rename.
- Change the name of the scene.
- Click Save Changes.
- Add hotspots that users will use to navigate the panorama.

- Select the thumbnail to select the scene.
- Rotate the scene to the part you want to place a hotspot.
- Select the Hotspot icon.
- Link to the scene.
- Select the scene you want to link to. This can be a website or another photo.
- Select icon or link to scene in website.
- Enter website URL and name that link description and select icon.
- Click Create.
- You can change the thumbnail for the scene if wanted.
- Click Snapshot icon.
- Drag and rotate scene until you get what you want.
- Select the Snapshot button again.
- To share your tour on social media:
  - Click on the three dots (. . .).
  - Click Share.
  - Click on any Social Media icons to share.
- Adding your tour to a website:
  - Click on three dots (. . .).
  - Click Share.
  - Click on embed code button.
  - Select size.
  - Slide to determine direction of rotation.
  - Select between Auto, Show, Hide.
  - Click embed code and paste into web page.
- Adding music.
  - Click on the three dots (. . .).
  - Click Edit Tour.
  - Select background music
  - Upload MP3 file.

RoundMe
http://www.roundme.com

RoundMe has free Basic Accounts that allow for 15 uploads a week. You can create tours, and there is unlimited storage on the site. You can embed your tour into your website. You need to sign up to use RoundMe.

You can sign in with Facebook or Twitter, or create an account with e-mail.

To create a VR tour:

- Log in to your account.
- Click Create Tour.
- Drag and drop your images at the prompt.
- Wait for them to finish uploading before moving on.
- After upload is complete, you will be prompted to add title, description, and categories.
- You can add GPS coordinates if you wish.
- Display and share.
- To save, you must make your tour public.
- If you wish to keep your tour private, turn off Published.

Google VR Tour Creator
htttp://vr.google.com/tourcreator

- Use Google account to sign in.
- Click on New Tour.
- Add title and description.
- Upload cover image.
- Choose a category.
- Click Create.
- Add a scene.
- Use Google Street imagery or upload your own.
- Add another scene.
  - Find it.
  - Add a scene.
  - Add the title.
  - Add a description.
- Keep adding scenes as needed.
- Publish—choose Public or Unlisted.
- Share URL, web page, social media, embed code, e-mail, or VR viewer.
- To overlay images into your scene:
  - Click Edit the Scene.
  - Add a Point of Interest. This does not have to be a place. You can add any image you wish. These could even be book covers.

Creating Your Own Photosphere

Google Street View

You can easily create your own photosphere video to use for your tour with your own smartphone. Google Street View works with both Android and iPhone to create a 360° video to use.

- Open the Google Street View app on your device.
- Click on Private.
- Click the orange camera icon.
- You can link to external 360° cameras or import 360° photos. To create your own photosphere, click Camera.
- Hold your device close to your body. Be sure the device is recording vertically.
- You will see an orange dot. Point the camera to the orange dot, and hold the camera steady until the camera takes the picture.
- Rotate your camera slowly and pause at each orange dot. The camera will take the picture automatically.
- When all photos have been taken, click on the check mark to indicate that you are finished taking photos.
- Your photos will render automatically. It may take a few minutes.
- When the photosphere is ready, it will save to the camera roll.
- You can publish the photosphere, or you can keep it private if you wish.

Presentations

Presentations can be used to showcase books in many ways. Many people like to stick to using the tried-and-true PowerPoint presentation. PowerPoint has a long history of making presentations easy and understandable. Google Slides can also be used for presentations and have become the go-to presentation creator today. But there are many more presentation makers that can be used easily.

Here are some ideas for using presentations in book promotion:

- Use presentations to promote library events such as author visits or book club events.
- Use presentations to promote reading challenges.
- Use a character to promote a book.
- Create a presentation showcasing an author's work.

- Create a presentation of a scene from a book.
- Create a presentation of books in a genre.
- Create a presentation of the state book award nominees to entice students to read them.
- Presentations are a good way to promote thematic books or new books.

Presentations can be set in a kiosk to run in a loop. If you have an unused TV or computer, give them new life by using them as kiosks to show presentations. Digital picture frames can also show presentations in kiosk mode.

Buncee
https://app.edu.buncee.com

Buncee is a web-based user-friendly app that makes creating interactive multimedia presentation simple. You can use your own content or import content from other sources. It also has an iOS app. (See Figure 2.10)
To create a Buncee:

- Sign up with your e-mail, your Google account, or your Microsoft account.
- You will be asked your role the first time you log in (Teacher/Student).
- To begin, click on the plus sign.
- Name your project.
- Add a background.
  - Buncee has built-in backgrounds you can choose from.
  - Solid color.
  - Web search for backgrounds.
  - Upload your own photos.
- Select items for your project by clicking the plus sign.
  - Text.
  - Stickers.
  - Message.
  - Web image.
  - Drawing.
  - Animation.
  - Photo.
  - YouTube video.

Figure 2.10 Buncee

- Tap on the item to insert.
- Drag the item to move on the slide, and adjust size and orientation.
- If you want to add another slide, click the plus sign.
  - Edit the next slide and any additional slides to complete your presentation.
- Share to your social media.
- Save to your camera roll.

Additional Uses of Buncee

Buncee is a multiuse app that can be used in a variety of ways other than just presentation.

- Digital or print signage.
- Digital or print flyers.
- Embed into web pages.
- Newsletters.
- Posters (create a QR code to generate a shortcut to the presentation).

ThingLink
http://www.thinglink.com

ThingLink offers free educational accounts. If you wish to have a classroom account for your students to use, you need to upgrade to the paid account. It is available as browser-based, iOS and Android. You can log in with Google account or create an account using your e-mail address.

To create an interactive photo using ThingLink:

- Sign into your account.
- Click Create.
- Upload an image, or take a photo using the device camera and save it to the camera roll.
- Add the title of the photo.
- On the photo, tap on an area of the photo that you want to make a link. You can link to text box, photo, URL, or YouTube video. These links are called nubbins.
- When you are finished adding the nubbins, preview your photo.
- When finished, you can:
  - Embed.
  - Link.
  - Link to social media.

When the viewer taps on a link, the text, photo, web page, or video will appear.

Adobe Spark Page
http://spark.adobe.com

Adobe Spark Page is available on iOS and Android. You can create a free account. Sign up with your Google account or Facebook account, or create a new account using your e-mail.

Steps for creating follow:

- Log in to your account.
- Click on the plus sign and choose Page.
- Add a title.
- After the title is completed, click on the plus sign to add to your page.
- You can insert text, video, or pictures.
- Upload your own photos or find photos through Adobe.
- Click plus sign to add another section.
- Scroll down to next section.
- Continue adding sections until your project is complete.
- Adobe supplies the credits for photos that are added.

- When finished, click Share.
- A link will be created. Use the link to add your video to your web page or social media.

Videos are used in a variety of ways to create a buzz for books. Use the videos on your web page to entice remote visitors to read. Add the videos to your social media pages to reach those viewers. If you have a digital picture frame or TV, add the videos to those and set them to continuous play mode to rotate through a few different videos. There are as many uses as you can think of. Try a few different apps to create your videos and see where it brings you. Save your videos for reuse in the future.

CHAPTER THREE

Audio

Podcasts

Podcasts are very popular and surprisingly easy to produce. Many libraries have a podcast for their library that features book selections, new books, interviews with authors, and other topics. Podcasts let listeners feel connected. And they are fun and informative.

Planning is one of the most important things in your podcast. You need to decide the length of the show. Short podcasts may be more useful to highlight books than longer podcasts. This is especially true for children who may have a shorter attention span. Who will be the host of the show? The show can have a variety of hosts or one host who will record all the shows. You could even have children record some of the shows. Will there be more than one person speaking? If so, you should think carefully where microphones will be placed. Or will each person have their own microphone? Will there be guests?

You can storyboard the podcast to get a good idea of how it will be produced. Be sure to have a rough script written so you can keep track of what is being said. It is also easier to read from a script than to ad lib. Since this is an audio show, it is fine to just read from a script.

Will the show have a consistent focus through many shows? For instance, will the show just highlight new books or thematic book suggestions? Or will there be a different topic for each show. How often will the show be produced? Daily, weekly, monthly?

Voice Memo

Once you decide to begin a podcast, you might want to try a few episodes before you spend money on equipment or software. The easiest way to record a podcast is right on your smartphone.

- Open the Voice Memo app on the phone and use that to record your podcast.
- Record your episode.
- Practice several times until you are comfortable.
- Save on your phone.

The quality of the recording will not be high level but will be sufficient for what you are doing. You will need to find a site to host the podcast and perhaps create an RSS feed. More on this at the end of the chapter.

Vocaroo
http://vocaroo.com

Vocaroo bills itself as "the premier voice-recording service." It has been around since 2007 and is used by amateurs and professionals alike.
To use Vocaroo:

- Go to the web page. There is no need to sign in or create an account.
- You will need Adobe Flash running to use the app. You can right click on the icon to make sure Flash is running. If not, you may need to install it.
- When it is ready, click to record. You need to allow access to your microphone.
- When finished recording, click Stop.
- You can listen to your recording.
- You can then Retry if you are not happy with it.
- When you are happy with the recording, click Save.
- You will then get a URL for your recording. You can download from there.
- You will have an embed code that can be used for embedding the recording into your web page or social media.
- You can download as MP3, Ogg, FLAC, or WAV formats.
- Messages are deleted from the Vocaroo site after a few months. You are given a delete URL to use if you wish to delete the sound file after you download.

Vocaroo is a good way to record short voice-overs or messages to use in your book promotion efforts.

SoundCloud
http://soundcloud.com

SoundCloud is a free audio recorder that is available as a desktop app, iPad, and Android. You need to sign in to use SoundCloud. You can sign in with Facebook or create your own account.

- Log in to the Dashboard.
- Click on Record to create your episode. There is no time limit to the episode.
- When you finish recording, hit Stop.
- Review your podcast and record again if you want.
- Click Upload Your Recording button.
    - You can also upload a picture.
    - You might want to add a picture of your library, yourself, or a book cover.
- Give the episode a title and description.
- Under Type, put podcast.
- Decide if the settings will be private or public.
- Click Save.
- The episode is now on the Dashboard.
- Click Share, which will create a widget code, a link, or a WordPress code, or publish to social media.
- SoundCloud acts as a host site and creates the RSS feed.

Anchor.fm

Anchor.fm is a free sound recorder that can be used on the web, iPad, or Android. The advantage of using Anchor.fm is that you do not need to find a hosting site nor create your own RSS feed. Anchor takes care of it all. Anchor.fm is a community site that has thousands of podcasts that you can subscribe to as well as create your own.

To use Anchor.fm:

- Create an account or sign in from your Facebook account, your Twitter account, or your Google account.
- You will be guided in the steps to set up your profile.

- Profile:
    - Choose a name for your station. You will want to choose a name that reflects what your podcast is about. You can use your library name or your classroom name if you wish.
    - Create your station URL, which is usually the name of the channel or your name.
    - Write a description of your podcast to let your listeners know your intent. You are limited to 110 characters.
- Add your web page URL if you want. You can also add your Twitter handle or Facebook profile.
- Choose your color scheme.
- Save your profile.

Recording:

- Press and hold the microphone button. It will stop recording when you let go. You can also hold your phone up as if talking to someone and record your podcast. The recoding will stop when you lower your phone.
- Preview your audio clip.
- Redo the clip if necessary.
- When you are ready, click Done.
- Add a caption to the clip and confirm.
- Audio clip is uploaded and public.
- Audio clips are available for 24 hours only. After that, they are archived.
- To turn your audio clip into a podcast, click the episode tab.
- Select all the clips you want to be in your podcast and click Next.
- Give the episode a title and a description and click Publish.
- Your clips are now saved to your episode and will be available for longer than 24 hours.
- Share your station on your web page or on social media sites.
- Listeners simply click on the episode to listen to the full podcast.

Audacity
http://audacity.com

If you feel that you would like to have more control of your podcast, you can download software to use to do that. On Windows computers, the most common free audio editor is Audacity. This is a free download that has a great variety of editing capabilities. It is a free open-sourced application. When installing, you should also find and install a copy of Lame encoder. Lame makes it possible to save your file as an MP3 file. This is the most common format to use in podcasts.

After installation:

- Check that the input source is correct. You should use an external microphone for Audacity, so make sure that it is selected rather than the internal microphone. The internal microphone can be used, but the quality is not as high as with an external microphone.
- To create an audio recording:

  - Click the Record button.
  - The timeline will display in real time so you will be able to keep track of the length of your recording.
  - Click the Stop button to end the recording.
  - Click Play and review your recording.

Editing:

- There are many effects built in to Audacity. Play around with them to see which ones you may want to use. Fade In and Fade Out are good to use at the beginning and at the end of the podcast. You may also wish to use echo effect, amplify, and more.

Save:

- Save in MP3 format. There are various formats that you can use, but MP3 works in most web applications.
- Upload your file to your podcast host site and your RSS feed.
- If you use a Mac, you can download GarageBand to use. It is similar to Audacity. GarageBand is available as an iOS app as well as a desktop application.

Equipment You May Want to Purchase

Once you have decided that you do want to continue to create podcasts, you may want to invest in equipment to make your podcast higher quality.

- Microphone
- Pop filter
- Headphones

Hosting Options

Once you have recorded your audio file to be used as a podcast, you may need to find a host site to deliver those files to your listeners. Sound-Cloud and Anchor.fm host the files for you, but if you want more control of where your files are stored and how they are delivered, there are many free hosting options.

Your Library Web Page

If your library or classroom has storage for you to use, you can upload your audio files onto the server and link to them on your web page.

Google Drive
http://drive.google.com

Google Drive is a free service that gives you a good deal of storage. You can save your files onto your Google Drive. You will need to add links to those audio files on your web page so your listeners can find them.

Podbean
http://podbean.com

Podbean is an easy-to-use podcast host that offers free access. Files cannot exceed 30 MB. There is a nice user interface and mobile options, and the RSS feed is created. Statistics are available to use.

Podomatic
http:www.podomatic.com

Podomatic is a free podcast host with easy-to-use interface. There is a limit of 15 GB of bandwidth each month. The limit for storage is 500 MB. You can create your podcast directly on the site or upload from your device.

Publishing on iTunes

Publishing your podcast on iTunes allows you to have listeners sub-scribe to your podcast.

- You must have an Apple ID to publish on iTunes.
- You will need to host your files on another site (e.g., Google Drive).
- You can design your cover image. This will be the album cover that users will see on iTunes. This might be a photo of your school or library. Or it could be a photo of you.
- Go to http://podcastsconnect.com.
- Click on the plus sign to add a new show.
- Enter the RSS feed URL for your podcast.
- Once the feed validates, click Submit.
- You will receive an e-mail from iTunes when your podcast feed is ready.

Voice Changers

When using apps that allow you to record your voice, you may want to change your voice to a character or to disguise your voice. There are dozens of voice changers available. Some have just a couple of choices for voice. Some have many, many choices including aliens and animals. A few web-based, free sites that are quick and easy to use are listed below.

Vozme
http://www.vozme.com

The Vozme site allows you to type in your text and then have it read in a different voice. The only choice is male/female. The voices are very mechanical sounding. When you are finished with text, choose Create. A rendering of the voice will load as an MP3 file. Simply download the MP3 file and upload the audio into your project.

Voice Changer Plus
http://voicechanger.io

Voice Changer Plus is a free site that does not require an account. When the site opens, choose a character for the voice. Click microphone button and record your voice. You can try out different voices without the need to rerecord. Save your file and enter a name for the recording. You can export the file to iCloud, Google Drive, OneDrive, or to a file. You can send the file to Facebook, Drive, or e-mail it.

Voice Spice
http://voicespice.com

Voice Spice is a free, web-based service. There are five different characters to choose from including a squirrel and a demon. You record into the app to create the voice. You can preview and rerecord if needed. Create your file and download when finished.

Audio book promotion is a great way to connect with kids on the go. Whereas both visual and video promotions require children to stop and interact with the information, audio promotions allow the children to keep going and still listen. These can be downloaded to listen to on long rides. They can be played over morning announcements at school. They can be played in long episodes or in short bursts. However you use audio book promotions, the children will benefit. Experiment with different delivery methods, and see if your kids are enticed to read more.

When trying to reach a variety of kids in your program, it is essential to hit different learning styles. Audio is a powerful way to reach kids. Audio can be used in morning announcements, on social media, or any variety of ways. There are so many ways to use audio to reach out and entice kids to want to read (or listen to) a book. How you use audio in your program is up to you.

CHAPTER FOUR

Resources

Book Trailers

Book trailers are like movie trailers as they act as video teasers for books. Creating book trailers can be done by using many of the apps that are included in this book. However, you may find book trailers that have already been created and posted to the Internet that can be used. You can embed them into web pages or link to them. Create looping videos to promote books in your collection. Be sure to credit the creators of the videos.

Here are a few places to find book trailers:

The Best YA Book Trailers of All Time
http://www.epicreads.com/blog/the-best-ya-book-trailers-of-all-time
This is a list of YA book trailers selected by TeamEpicReads for Epic! These are so good, they should be movies.

Book Trailers for All
http://www.youtube.com/user/booktrailers4all
This is a curated YouTube channel for book trailers. The trailers are appropriate for children up through high school.

Book Trailers for Readers
http://www.youtube.com/user/mhmediaspec
This site includes primarily book trailers for the Florida Sunshine State Young Reader Book Awards. The books are popular, so they can be used on other sites.

Book Trailers: Movies for Literacy
http://homepages.dsu.edu/mgeary/booktrailers
The page includes book trailers for elementary grades. There are separate lists for late elementary and adolescent books.

Candlewick Press YouTube Channel
http://www.youtube.com/channel/UCOp4BcxCLcjf2K4-zOR9c0A
The web page includes many book trailers created by Candlewick Press for their books.

Digital Booktalk
http://www.digitalbooktalk.net
K12 video book trailers created by students from the University of Central Florida.

Harper Teen YouTube Channel
http://www.youtube.com/user/HarperKids
Book trailers created by Harper Teen to promote their books.

Houghton Mifflin Harcourt YouTube Channel
http://www.youtube.com/user/HMHCoTV
A collection of book trailers from Houghton Mifflin Harcourt to promote their books.

Little Brown Young Readers YouTube Channel
http://www.youtube.com/channel/UC13E3aSIWXo4_L4SvfuBlkA
The YouTube channel from Little Brown Young Readers. The channel includes many book trailers promoting their books.

Naomi Bates's Digital Book Talks
http://fisdbooktrailers.pbworks.com/w/page/31449210/Secondary -Book-Trailers
A shared repository of book trailers from school district.

Pima County Public Library Trailer
http://www.library.pima.gov/blogs/post/watch-the-trailer-read-the -book
Book trailers curated by the Pima Library.

Simon and Schuster Books YouTube Channel
http://www.youtube.com/channel/UC76b6XAkcfMLqgCV4xBuoTQ
The YouTube channel by Simon and Schuster Books. The book trials showcase books for school-age children.

Slimekids BookTrailers
http://www.slimekids.com/book-trailers
Slimekids features an extensive collection of book trailers organized by year and grade level. The site is maintained by Andy Fine, parent and teacher.

YouTube Book Lounge Channel
http://www.youtube.com/user/BookLounge
YouTube channel of Penguin Random House Canada. There are book trailers for books for all ages.

Thematic Book Lists

Looking for books that include scenes from a tea party? Want to do a program on farm animals? Doing a newsletter about a holiday? Or celebrating Black History Month on your blog? It is great to find a thematic list on the Internet as a place to begin our activity. These can be featured on web pages or social media.

- Thematic lists make great displays for the library or classroom.
- Use them in animated videos or photos.
- Use them in contests and book quizzes.
- Use them in memes.
- Use them in theme promotions.

Some web pages that are available on the Internet are:

ATN Reading Lists
http://sites.google.com/site/atnreadinglists/home
Maintained by Nancy Keane. Book list suggestions are culled from discussions on professional e-mail lists. The site is a collaborative and members add book list as well. There are more than 2,000 thematic lists.

Book Rio
http://bookriot.com
Dedicated to the idea of writing about books and reading books. Some of the writers are pros, but many are not. They accept book reviews and book lists from the field. Book lists cover a variety of topics and interest levels.

Brightly
http://www.readbrightly.com
Brightly was created in 2014 by a team of bookworms and parents. It launched in partnership with Penguin Random House. The site offers book suggestions for every age and stage.

Canadian Children's Book Council Themed Book Lists
http://bookcentre.ca/resources/themed-book-lists
The Canadian Children's Book Centre is a national, not-for-profit organization. Their charge is to encourage, promote, and support reading, writing, illustrating, and publishing Canadian books for young readers.

CCBC Booklists
http://ccbc.education.wisc.edu/books/bibBio.asp
The CCBC (Cooperative Children's Book Center, University of Wisconsin–Madison) has created bibliographies and book lists of recommended books for babies, elementary students, middle school students, and high school students. The site is indexed and can be searched.

Lee & Low Book Lists by Theme
http://www.leeandlow.com/educators/books-by-theme
Lee & Low is the largest multicultural children's book publisher in the United States. They are committed to diversity in children's books.

Miss Rumphius Effect
http://missrumphiuseffect.blogspot.com/p/thematic-book-lists.html
Blog maintained by an educator dealing with children's literature.

Mrs. ReaderPants Book Lists
http://www.readerpants.net/p/thematic-lists.html
Book recommendations for middle and high school students by Mrs. ReaderPants (Leigh Collazo).

Read & Shine
http://www.readandshine.com/category/reading-lists
Professionally curated reading lists developed by topic and/or age level. Some reading lists include titles from multiple age groups and will appear under more than one category.

Ready-to-Go Book Lists for Teachers
http://www.scholastic.com/teachers/collections/2017/ready-go-book
-lists-teachers

New titles and fresh teaching ideas in book lists organized by author, holiday, topic, and genre by Scholastic.

Thematic Book Lists by TeachingBooks.net
http://www.teachingbooks.net/tb.cgi?go=1&isAdv=1&keyword_type1=list&list_type=thematic_booklist
TeachingBooks.net is a subscription service dedicated to giving children and teachers the resources they need to connect with books on a personal level. The site offers lots of free pages for those not subscribed to the service. The book lists are one of those services.

Thematic Book Reviews
http://www.apples4theteacher.com/languagearts/books/thematic-books.html
Apples4thteacher.com offers many resources for teachers to use with reading. The thematic lists have been compiled to help teachers pull together a well-rounded unit of study by theme.

Themed Book Lists by Reading Rockets
http://www.readingrockets.org/books/booksbytheme
The themed book lists have been selected by Maria Salavadore for children up to 9 years old.

YALSA Booklists
http://www.ala.org/yalsa/booklistsawards/booklists
The Young Adults Library Services Association (YALSA) selects the best books and media for teens. Whether you're looking for a book for a reluctant or avid teen reader, there's sure to be a title that will fit the bill.

Books in Series

One popular source of book promotion is books in series. Series books are very popular, and many children can't wait to get the next one. But have you ever tried to create a book promotion for a book series but didn't know if you had all of them? Have children asked for the latest series book but didn't know the title? Have you ever tried to figure out a complicated series to be sure you have them all? There are several good resources that can help you with series books.

Books in Series Order
http://www.bookseriesinorder.com

The goal of this website is to provide information about children's books in series. It provides the book series on order by author and then in order of the character.

Fantastic Fiction
http://www.fantasticfiction.com
Fantastic Fiction includes books from more than 40,000 authors. These are not all children's books; adult science fiction books are also included.

FictFact
http://www.fictfact.com
FictFact will keep track of the books you're reading and give you a list of the books you need to read next. You'll be able to find users with similar tastes, tag books and series, and get recommendations on other book series. They'll even e-mail you the week books you're following come out.

Follett Titlewave (need free subscription)
http://www.titlewave.com
Follett Titlewave is the online book catalog for Follett books. The subscriptions are limited to librarians and educators. Once you have an account, you will find a plethora of information that allows you to access a database of books in series, and you can create your own lists.

Kent District Library What's Next
http://ww2.kdl.org/libcat/whatsnext.asp
Kent District Library maintains a searchable database of series books. They include both adult and youth books. Simply put your author or series in the database, and you will be brought to a listing of all books in the series.

Mid-Continent Public Library Juvenile Series & Sequels
http://www.mymcpl.org/books-movies-music/read/juvenile-series -and-sequels
MCPL maintains a database of juvenile series and sequels that contains more than 36,000 books in 4,900 series. Series can be viewed by series title, series subjects, book title, and book author.

Nebraska Library Commission Books in Series
http://www.nlc.state.ne.us/ref/booksinseries.asp
This database is created and maintained by the Nebraska Library Commission. You can search by author, book title, or series title.

Order of Books
http://www.orderofbooks.com
The site claims to be a complete list of books in series. The database includes juvenile books and adult books.

Books to Movies

Some of the best children's and YA books have been made into movies. Children often debate which is better—the book or the movie. Promote books that have been made into movies using the apps throughout this book. Or you may want to promote upcoming movies that have been adapted from books. Read the book before the movie is released. (Please note: The URL for some of these lists may change when they update their lists.)

Here are a few places to find movie adaptations of books:

11 YA Books Being Made into Movies That You Need to Read ASAP
http://rivetedlit.com/2018/07/25/books-being-made-into-movies
This is a list by Simon Teen that showcases their books that are being made into movies.

21 Hot YA Novels to Read before They're Movies
http://www.popsugar.com/entertainment/YA-Novels-Becoming -Movies-34609728
An overview of YA books being made into movies from Popsugar.

The 40 Best Book-to-Film Adaptations Ever
http://www.shortlist.com/entertainment/films/40-best-film-adap tations/84766
This list does not limit itself to upcoming films. It is an overview of some of the best adaptations.

Goodreads Book-to-Film Book Lists
http://www.goodreads.com/list/tag/book-to-film
Book lists created by members of Goodreads. Some of the lists look at movies that have already come out, but others highlight upcoming films.

Goodreads YA Novels Made into Movies
http://www.goodreads.com/list/show/2241.YA_Novels_Made_Into _Movies

Book lists created by members that showcase YA books that have been made into movies.

Movie Insider
http://www.movieinsider.com
Track upcoming movies through all stages of production.

Movies Based on Books' Common Sense Media
http://www.commonsensemedia.org/lists/movies-based-on-books
From Common Sense Media, this list includes past films as well as upcoming films.

MovieWeb
http://movieweb.com/movies/2020
MovieWeb lists movies that are coming out over the next few years. Not all of them are based on books.

New Movies Coming Soon on IMDB.com
http://www.imdb.com/movies-coming-soon/?ref_=nv_mv_cs
The IMDB listing of movies based on books coming to the theater soon. This includes both adult and children's movies.

PBS Books' Big List of Book-to-Movie Adaptations
http://www.pbs.org/book-view-now/blogs/news/2018/03/01/book-adaptations
Compiled by PBS, this is a listing of children's books that are being made into movies.

TV Shows Based on Books
http://www.commonsensemedia.org/lists/tv-shows-based-on-books
From Common Sense Media, this database includes television shows that are based on books.

Book Widgets

A widget is a stand-alone application that can be embedded into third party sites by any user on a page where they have rights of authorship, for example, a web page, blog, or profile on a social media site.

JacketFlap Book Widgets
http://www.jacketflap.com/widgets.asp

JacketFlap's Book Widgets are a powerful way to spread the word about great children's books. You can install these widgets on your blog or website in less than a minute.

Google Books
http://books.google.com
Search for a book in Google Books. Most offer a preview of the book. You will find an embed code that will allow you to put the preview on your web page.

GoodReads
http://www.goodreads.com
Widgets are a way to show off what you are reading on your blog or on any other website you have.

HarperCollins Browse Inside
http://browseinside.harpercollins.com
With Browse Inside, you can try before you buy! Browse Inside is just like flipping through the pages of a book at your favorite bookshop, but better!

You can use the embed code to add Browse Inside to your web page.

First Lines

One way to entice students into wanting to know more and perhaps pick up a book is to tease them with the first line of a book. So many first lines are sure to make them want to know more.

- These lines can be embedded into web pages or social media.
- They make great displays for the library or classroom.
- Use them in animated videos or photos.
- Combine book covers and first lines to create posters.
- Use them in contests and book quizzes.
- There are so many ways to use the first lines.

Here are some websites that include some of the best first lines from children's books:

21 of the Best Opening Lines in Children's Books
http://www.weareteachers.com/21-of-the-best-opening-lines-in-childrens-books

100 Best Opening Lines in Children's Books
http://www.stylist.co.uk/books/100-best-opening-lines-from-child
rens-books/125320

Barnes and Noble Best Opening Lines in YA Books
http://www.barnesandnoble.com/blog/teen/15-of-the-best-opening
-lines-in-ya

Hook, Line and Sinker: The Best Opening Lines in Children's and Young Adult Fiction
http://www.theguardian.com/childrens-books-site/2016/jan/01/best
-opening-lines-childrens-and-young-adult-fiction

NPR Great Opening Lines
http://www.npr.org/2007/06/25/11260800/great-opening-lines-to
-hook-young-readers

Opening Lines in Picture Books
http://www.childrensbookacademy.com/blogfish/july-20th-2014

New and Forthcoming Books

Some young readers look forward to new books and want to know what is coming out. You can create a display that creates a buzz for new books and those that are coming out soon. Using some of these titles increases anticipation for them. They also may lead to children requesting similar titles to read while they wait for the book to be published.

Epic Reads Coming Soon
http://www.epicreads.com/books/index/sort/comingSoon
A database of YA books that are coming out soon or are recent releases. Search by genre.

Harper Collins Coming Soon
http://harpercollinschildrens.com/Parents/BookFinder/ComingSoon
.aspx
Books being published by HarperCollins that will be coming out soon.

Penguin Random House Children's Books Coming Soon
http://www.penguinrandomhouse.com/books/coming-soon-childrens

Children's books being published by Penguin Random House that will be coming out soon.

Penguin Random House Teen Books Coming Soon
http://www.penguinrandomhouse.com/books/coming-soon-teen -young-adult
Teen books being published by Penguin Random House that will be coming out soon.

Publishers Weekly New Titles
http://www.publishersweekly.com/pw/by-topic/new-titles/childrens -announcements/index.html
This is a listing of children's books coming soon and includes their release dates. This is not limited to one publisher.

Simon and Schuster Coming Soon
http://www.simonandschuster.com/search/books/Coming-Soon/_/N-i7o
Children's books being published by Simon and Schuster that will be coming out soon.

TeenReads Coming Soon
http://www.teenreads.com/coming-soon
From The Book Report; lists teen books that are coming out soon. This is not limited by publisher.

Young Adult Book Release Dates
http://yalit.com
A compilation of YA books that will be published soon.

Literary Quotes

There are many wonderful quotes from children's books that can be used in your book promotions. Some of the quotes are well known and can peek a child's interest in a book. Others are inspirational and can be used in many situations. Use these in your program to celebrate authors and books.

- These can be embedded into web pages or social media.
- They make great displays for the library or classroom.
- Use them in animated videos or photos.

- Use them in contests and book quizzes.
- Use them in memes.
- Use them in daily announcements.

Some web pages that are available on the Internet are:

9 Quotes about Love from Children's Books
http://www.scholastic.com/parents/books-and-reading/raise-a-reader
-blog/9-quotes-about-love-childrens-books.html

10 Profound Children's Book Quotes That Probably Changed Your Life
http://parade.com/276198/linzlowe/10-profound-childrens-book
-quotes-that-probably-changed-your-life

10 Uplifting Quotes from Your Favorite Children's Books
http://www.goodnet.org/articles/10-uplifting-quotes-from-your
-favorite-childrens-books

15 Important Pieces of Wisdom from Children's Books
http://www.radiotimes.com/news/2015-12-26/15-important-pieces-of
-wisdom-found-in-childrens-books

19 Best Children's Book Quotes
http://www.readbrightly.com/19-best-childrens-book-quotes

20 Best Children's Book Quotes of All Time
http://www.redbookmag.com/life/mom-kids/advice/g598/classic
-childrens-books-quotes

27 Classic Children's Book Quotes Every Adult Needs to Hear
http://www.rd.com/culture/childrens-book-quotes

Best Children's Book Quotes
http://bookriot.com/2017/10/30/best-childrens-books-quotes

The Greatest Inspirational Quotes from Children's Books
http://www.theguardian.com/childrens-books-site/2016/jan/21/the
-greatest-inspirational-quotes-from-childrens-books

Quotable Reading Quotes
http://www.readingrockets.org/books/fun/quotable

Royalty-Free Music for Projects

When creating projects for book promotion, you may want to use music or sound effects to enhance your promotion. Think about the music or sounds that you want for your book promotion. What kind of mood do you want to create? Mysterious? Happy? Serious? Do you want music that has words, or that is just instrumental? If you choose a song with words, are they appropriate for the book you are promoting? Will they detract from your message? Will people be listening and singing the song rather than concentrating on your book promotion? Or will that make your promotion better?

When you have determined what sounds you need, you need to be sure you have the rights to use that sound. Most music on the Internet is protected under copyright laws. Your use for internal promotions may be covered under fair use. Many audios may be used under Creative Commons licensing. Always check before using.

Some sites that are good to use to find sounds for your project include:

BBC Sound Effects
http://bbcsfx.acropolis.org.uk
These 16,000 BBC Sound Effects are made available by the BBC in WAV format to download for use under the terms of the RemArc license. The sound effects are BBC copyright, but they may be used for personal, educational, or research purposes, as detailed in the license. So, if you are looking for the sound of an MRI or a croquette match, this is your place to look.

Free Play Music
http://freeplaymusic.com
You can search by style and mood. If you use this site, save the file as MP3.

Getty Free Music
http://www.gettyimages.com/music
Royalty-free music. High-quality music and audio clips, all with flexible, easy-to-understand usage rights.

Incompetech
http://incompetech.com/m/c/royalty-free
Incompetech includes music by Kevin MacLeod that is royalty-free. It lets you customize your search by feel, genre, tempo, or length.

Jamendo
http://www.jamendo.com
Discover free music downloads and streaming from thousands of independent artists. Explore new songs every day, create your own playlists, and share.

Melody Loops
http://melodyloops.com
Get a multiuse license and download royalty-free background music. Enjoy a wonderful selection of melodies for your use.

Partners in Rhyme
http://www.partnersinrhyme.com/pir/free_music_loops.shtml
They can only give permission for the use of sound effects they create: spoken words and phrases, weird sound effects, MIDI music loops, musical instruments, strange human sounds, button clicks and beeps, odd animal sounds, and ambient environments.

Royalty-Free Music from Soundcloud
http://soundcloud.com/royalty-free-audio-loops
Royalty-free music loops, wide range genre and style. Music licensing.

WavSource
http://www.wavsource.com/sfx/sfx.htm
Download these sounds. Do *not* link directly to them on the web page as they won't work. They must be saved locally as WAV files.

QR Codes

A QR (quick response) code is a type of 2D bar code that is used to provide easy access to information through a smartphone or tablet. A QR reader app needs to be installed on the smartphone. The smartphone camera is pointed at the QR code, which will open content. Any digital content can be linked to a QR code. There are QR generators that allow you to create your own free QR codes. QR codes are free to use and never expire.

Create your own QR code with:

Chrome Extension
Generates a QR code from the page URL of the current tab with a single click. The QR code is displayed inline in a small pop-up.

GoQRME
http://goqr.me

Just enter your text or your URL. The QR code will be generated automatically as you type. Just click on the Download button to get the created QR code image. You can embed the QR code directly on your own website and use it; just have a look at the code offered by the Embed button. Of course, you can place and use the QR graphic on leaflets, posters, books, or other products without any costs/for free, including commercial use.

QR Code Generator
http://qrcode.kaywa.com

QR codes come in two types, either static or dynamic. We always recommend using dynamic codes. Static codes simply encode the information. With Kaywa you can create an unlimited number of static QR codes free of charge.

QR Monkey
http://www.qrcode-monkey.com

Easy-to-use QR code creator. In addition to creating your QR code, you can set colors, add a logo image, or choose to customize the design.

QR Stuff
http://www.qrstuff.com

Create QR codes for more than 20 data types and smartphone actions.

Passive Reader's Advisory

It is great when children come to us looking for book suggestions, and we can have an interactive discussion with them. This often creates the best way to connect kids with books that they will enjoy. But often children don't feel comfortable asking for ideas of what they should read. There are a variety of reasons for this. They may be in a hurry and don't want to answer a lot of questions about what they like to read. They may feel uncomfortable talking with someone they don't know. They just may not feel like interacting. They may not be able to get to the library to talk to someone in person. Whatever the reason, using tech tools helps to connect.

Some ideas for using technology include:

Displays

As much as we may not want to believe it, children often choose a book by its cover. Displays can be thematic or have a common look to them—for instance, books that all have a snow globe on the cover or are all the same color. Book displays are eye catching in the library, but for those who can't see them in person, you can use technology to share the displays through photographs or videos added to the Internet.

Bookmarks

Children love bookmarks. You can certainly purchase lovely bookmarks from vendors, but you can also use technology to create your own. Use bookmarks to showcase thematic book lists, lists of books nominated for state awards, or read-alike books. Again, for those who can't come to the library to pick up the bookmark, you can share them through social media or web pages. Size them on your web page so children can print them and cut them out to use.

Sticky Notes

Use brightly colored sticky notes to bring attention to a book. You can write a recommendation on the sticky note and put them on books to draw attention to them. Using technology, you can add digital sticky notes to book covers to make those stand out.

Reading Suggestion Portals

ALA Youth Media Awards
http://www.ala.org/awardsgrants/awards
Each year, the American Library Association awards medals for the best book in a variety of categories. Books for all ages are included. The lists for each award include the criteria for the award and the current winners.

Any New Books?
http://www.anynewbooks.com
Any New Books is a free notification service that was developed to alert you to new books in categories of your choice. The selection process is not

automated, because we believe a human editor is better able to pick books that will better appeal to a wide audience.

ATN Reading Lists
http://sites.google.com/site/atnreadinglists/home
ATN Reading Lists was started in 1996 and includes thematic reading lists for books from PK to 12. The lists are culled from professional resources and from librarian members. There is a large selection of read-alike books that offer suggestions on what to read when you loved a particular book.

BookBrowse
http://www.bookbrowse.com
BookBrowse is an online magazine for booklovers—including reviews, previews, "beyond the book" articles, author interviews, reading guides, and much more.

Book Riot
http://www.bookriot.com
Book Riot is dedicated to the idea that writing about books and reading should be just as diverse as books and readers are. So sometimes we are serious and sometimes silly. The site includes book reviews, podcasts, reading lists, and more.

BookSeer
http://www.bookseer.com
Simply enter the title and author of a book you liked, and it will give you suggestions for other books you may want to try.

Booktalks—Quick and Simple
http://www.nancykeane.com/booktalks
This site includes more than 10,000 ready-to-use book talks to use with grades K–12. The books have mostly one book talk per title, but more popular books may have several book talks for the same book. The book talks are available to use free of charge. Use them as is or as an inspiration for your own program.

Brightly
http://readbrightly.com
Founded in 2014 by a small team of passionate bookworms and parents, Brightly is a resource to help moms, dads, and educators grow lifelong

readers. The website features book recommendations from all publishers for every age and stage, reading tips and insights, seasonal inspirations, author essays, contests, gift guides, and more.

Carnegie Public Library Book Lists
http://www.carnegielibrary.org/kids-teens-booklists
Book lists curated by the staff of the Carnegie Public Library. Look around to find some interesting books to try.

Denver Public Library Book Lists for Kids and Teens
http://teens.denverlibrary.org/books/lists
The Denver Public Library has recommendations for books to read. There are separate lists from children and teens.

Genrefluent
http://genrefluent.com
Curated by Diana Trixier Herald, this blog offers recommendations in all genres.

Goodreads
http://goodreads.com
Goodreads is a social networking site for bookworms from all over to share the books they are reading and recommend books for others.

Graphic Novel Reporter
http://www.graphicnovelreporter.com
Part of the Book Report network, this site is all things graphic novels. There are recommendations, author interviews, and more.

Guys Read
http://guysread.com
Jon Scieszka started Guys Read to showcase books that have boy appeal. This site is undergoing reconstruction as of fall 2018.

HarperChildrens
http://harpercollins.com/childrens
HarperChildrens maintains a database of suggestions for good children's books.

HarperTeen
http://harpercollins.com/teen-bestsellers

HarperTeen curated site to showcase the best of their teen books.

JacketFlap
http://www.jacketflap.com
JacketFlap is a resource that connects you to the work of more than 200,000 authors, illustrators, publishers, and other creators of books for children and young adults.

Jim Trelease's Home Page
http://trelease-on-reading.com
Jim Trelease is a strong advocate of self-selected independent reading. His site is filled with ideas for reading programs, books lists, and much more.

Kids@random.com
http://rhcbooks.com
Random House catalog on books on their front list. Recommendations are divided into Babies & Toddlers, Beginning Readers, Intermediate Readers, and Young Adults.

Literature-Map
http://literature-map.com
The Literature-Map is part of Gnod, the Global Network of Discovery. It is based on Gnooks, Gnod's literature recommendation system. The more people like an author and another author, the closer together these two authors will move on the Literature-Map.

Love Reading 4 Kids
http://lovereading4kids.co.uk
A team of bookworms set up this book recommendation site to help people find their next favorite book.

A Mighty Girl Reads
http://www.amightygirl.com
A Mighty Girl is the "world's largest collection of books, toys, movies, and music for parents, teachers, and others dedicated to raising smart, confident, and courageous girls and, of course, for girls themselves!"

Multnomah County Library Series and Sequels
http://www.mymcpl.org/books-movies-music/read/juvenile-series
-and-sequels
The juvenile series and sequels database contains more than 36,000 books in 4,900 series titles that are classified into three audiences:

juvenile easy (birth through 2nd grade), juvenile (2nd through 6th grade), and young adult (6th through 12th grade).

No Flying No Tights: Graphic Novels for Teens
http://www.noflyingnotights.com
An in-depth resource for librarians about comics and graphic novels.

NYPL's Recommendations
http://www.nypl.org/collections/nypl-recommendations/lists
A listing of book lists created just for you by NYPL's librarians.

Read.gov
http://www.read.gov
The Center for the Book in the Library of Congress invites people of all ages to discover the fascinating people, places, and events that await you whenever you read.

Reading Rants!
http://www.readingrants.org
A group of book lists for teens who need a good read but are wondering if there's life after John Green and J. K. Rowling.

Riffle
http://www.rifflebooks.com
Riffle is a vibrant community of book lovers, librarians, bloggers, educators, publishers, authors, booksellers, and avid readers. Riffle inspires people to read more books by connecting them with others who love the same things.

Simon and Schuster Books for Kids
http://www.simonandschuster.com/kids
Book suggestions from Simon and Schuster Publisher. The books are divided into interest level: baby to age 3, ages 4–8, ages 9–11, and ages 12 and up.

Simon and Schuster Books for Teens
http://simonandschuster.com/teen
Book suggestions from Simon and Schuster Publisher especially for teens.

Tales Told Tall
http://talestoldtall.com

Librarian Michael Sullivan reviews books that boys will enjoy.

Teen Book Finder
http://booklists.yalsa.net
Search 4,000+ books, audiobooks, and films from YALSA's book awards and book lists.

TeenReads
http://teenreads.com
Part of the Book Report network, the sites includes reviews of new teen books.

Teens@Random (Random House)
http://www.randomhouse.com/teens
Random House publisher's website of teen books.

We Need Diverse Books
http://diversebooks.org
The goal of WNDB is putting more books featuring diverse characters into the hands of all children.

What Should I Read Next?
http://www.whatshouldireadnext.com
Enter a book you like, and the site will analyze the huge database of real readers' favorite books to provide book recommendations and suggestions for what to read next.

What's Next Database
http://ww2.kdl.org/libcat/whatsnext.asp
What's Next®: Books in series database helps you search series fiction.

YA Book Shelf
http://www.yabookshelf.com
Whether you have a craving for werewolves, vampires, or other realistic fiction, YA Book Shelf will help you find the books that generate a lot of buzz, some favorites that we can't forget from our own YA years, and everything in between.

YALSA Book Lists and Awards
http://ala.org/yalsa/book-media-lists

Teen Book Finder Database, which is a one-stop shop for finding selected lists and award winners. Users can search this free resource by award, list name, year, author, genre, and more, as well as print customizable lists.

Book Suggestion Apps

Book Wizard

iOS and Android.
Instantly get levels for Guided Reading, Lexile® Measure, DRA, or Grade Level from the Book Wizard database of 50,000 children's books.

Libby

iOS and Android.
You can access e-books and audiobooks from your local library. It has thousands of e-books and audiobooks you can borrow, instantly, for free, using just the device in your hand.

Library Extension

Chrome.
If your library uses this app, you can add it to your Chrome browser, and it will check the holdings of the public library that match your search.

Teen Book Finder

iOS and Android.
YALSA's Teen Book Finder is a free online database and app to help teens, parents, librarians and library staff, educators, and anyone who loves YA literature access nearly 4,000 titles, recognized YALSA's awards, and YALSA's lists on their smartphone.

We Read Too

iOS and Android.
We Read Too is a directory of hundreds of picture, chapter, middle grade, and young adult books written by authors of color featuring main characters of color. Whether you are a parent, librarian, teacher, or student,

We Read Too is the best resource for you to find diverse books for young readers.

Free Audiobooks

Audiobooks are a good way to get children into books. They can listen to the book without having to read along. Or, if they wish, they can read along. There are many resources for audiobooks. Many libraries subscribe to a service like OverDrive, which provides their patrons with free access.

There are many sources of free audiobooks available on the Internet.

LearnOutLoud.com
http://www.learnoutloud.com/Free-Audiobooks
Download thousands of the best free audiobooks online through Learn OutLoud.com.

LibriVox
http://librivox.org
LibriVox volunteers record chapters of books in the public domain and then release the audio files back onto the net for free. All audios are in the public domain and are free to use.

Lit2Go (stories and poems)
http://etc.usf.edu/lit2go
Lit2Go offers audiobooks, plays, short stories, and poems that have been tailored for use in classrooms. Along with each free audiobook, you'll get citation information, play time, and word count.

Loyal Books (formerly Books Should Be Free)
http://www.loyalbooks.com
Loyal Books shares free audiobooks from titles in the public domain.

Storyline
http://www.storylineonline.net
Books read by Screen Actors Guild members.

Storynory
http://www.storynory.com

Storynory has been giving free audio stories to the world since November 2005. A podcast and a website with audio streaming.

Finding E-books

Finding e-books to share is becoming much easier with more booksellers providing access to them. Libraries are also providing online access to e-books through their digital collections.

DailyLit
http://www.dailylit.com
DailyLit offers public domain e-books delivered in daily installments. You can receive the daily updates by email or RSS feed. The first two books offered were *Pride and Prejudice* and *War of the Worlds*.

Feedbooks
http://www.feedbooks.com
This French e-book site is tailored for mobile browsers, so you can download free e-books directly to your tablet or smartphone. Feedbooks offers thousands of public domain e-books in five languages.

Google Book Search
http://books.google.com
Search books on Google Book Search and you will get the results for that book. Look for Full View link and you just may find the full text of the book that can be read in your browser.

International Children's Digital Literature
http://en.childrenslibrary.org
This is a free online library of digitized children's books in 59 languages. The site serves children from ages 3 to 13 from around the world.

Internet Archives
http://archive.org/details/texts
The website is a huge repository of text, audio, and video files, including public domain titles. You can browse and read online more than 5 million books and items from more than 1,500 collections. The collections include the Library of Congress, American libraries, Canadian libraries, books from Project Gutenberg, and from the Million Books Project, as well as books for children. On the Internet Archive you will find book files in more than 180 languages.

Kindle Owners' Lending Library
http://www.amazon.com

Prime members can borrow one book from Kindle Owners' Lending Library each calendar month. You can download the book to compatible devices registered to the same Amazon account or to the account of adults in the same Amazon household.

Loyal Books
http://www.loyalbooks.com

There are thousands of free public domain e-books and audiobooks available. Titles in 30 languages are available. The site was formerly called Books Should Be Free.

Open Library
http://openlibrary.org

There are more than 1,000,000 free e-book titles available. Most of the titles are in the public domain, but you can also find here a growing lending library of more than 200,000 contemporary e-books.

OverDrive
http://overdrive com

OverDrive is a service offered by public and school libraries to their patrons. You can access OverDrive through their web page and download both e-books and audiobooks directly online. The books are checked out for a predetermined period of time and will automatically be wiped from your device when the time is up. Libraries can determine their own collections and checkout time limits. The Libby app can be downloaded onto your device to make the checkout procedure very easy.

Public Domain E-books:

Project Gutenberg
http://www.gutenberg.org

Project Gutenberg offers more than 57,000 free e-books. Choose among free e-pub books, free Kindle books, download them, or read them online. You will find the world's great literature here, with focus on older works for which copyright has expired. Thousands of volunteers digitized and diligently proofread the e-books, for enjoyment and education.

YouTube

YouTube is a free resource to collect your videos for your book promotion projects. The easiest way for your users to find your content is to set up a YouTube channel. You can add a link to your channel on your promotional materials.

Setting Up a YouTube Channel

- Create a YouTube account if you don't have one.
- Sign into your account.
- Click on the user icon on the top right of the screen.
- Click on the gear icon to get to your account's settings.
- Click on Create a new channel,
- Click on Choose Use business or other name.
- Add your brand name and click Create.

YouTube Playlist

To highlight selected videos, you can set up a playlist in your YouTube channel.

- Open your YouTube channel.
- Create new playlist.
- Add title and description.
- Add videos by URL.
- Paste to add.
- Keep going to add as many as you want.
- You can reorder the playlist even after videos have been added.
- Go to settings.
- Click Done.
- Share to social media.
- Embed on a web page.
- E-mail link.
- You can add more videos as needed.
- You can delete playlists and add more.

YouTube Alternatives

If you are worried about the content on YouTube and would like to publish on an alternative site, there are several to choose from.

Dailymotion
http://dailymotion.com
Very similar to YouTube in look and feel. It is easy to use and you can upload your videos. There is a 4-GB upload video limit, which means you can upload about 60 minutes of HD video.

Facebook Live
A fun, powerful way to connect with your followers. You can send notifications when you go live so your followers know to tune in to your broadcasts at the right time. After your live event, the video will be published on your Facebook page so that those who missed it can watch it later. You can remove the post when you no longer wish to have it available.

Flickr
http://www.filckr.com
In addition to hosting photos, Flickr also hosts short videos. There is a limit to 90-second videos, so this is a good location to host those short, on-the-fly videos.

MetaCafe
http://metacafe.com
MetaCafe has a 90-second limit on its videos. It is a good host for short, on-the-fly videos used in book promotion.

Vimeo
http://vimeo.com
There is a limit to 500 MB of content uploaded each week.

Children's Book Blogs

Feedspot Top 100 Children's Book Blogs for Parents, Teachers, and Kids
http://blog.feedspot.com/childrens_book_blogs
The rankings from Feedspot are determined using search and social metrics. These are the Top 100 blogs out of the thousands of children's blogs on the Internet. Reprinted with permission.

1. Kids Book Review
http://www.kids-bookreview.com
This blog was founded by Australian author/illustrator Tania McCartney. Contributors include authors, illustrators, and publishers.

2. Kidlit: How to Write and Publish Children's Books
http://kidlit.com
This blog is from Mary Kole, a former literary agent. She writes about children's literature and the writing process.

3. School Library Journal
http://www.slj.com
School Library Journal is one of the largest publications geared totally to school libraries. There are reviews for books for children, YA, and professionals.

4. The Horn Book by Bertha Mahony
http://www.hbook.com
The Horn Book blog is the online complement to *Horn Book Magazine*.

5. The Children's Book Review
http://www.thechildrensbookreview.com
This blog is a well-known blog devoted to writing about children's literature and literacy.

6. Chronicle Books Blog
http://www.chroniclebooks.com/blog
A companion blog to Chronicle Books publishing.

7. Lee & Low Blog: Exploring Children's Books through the Lens of Diversity
http://blog.leeandlow.com
Lee & Low is a book publisher devoted to diversity in children's literature. This blog highlights the issue of diversity in children's literature.

8. Jen Robinson's Book Page
http://jkrbooks.typepad.com
Author Jen Robinson shares the books she has read and her thoughts on children's literature.

9. Mr. Schu Reads: Exploring Children's Literature through Book Trailers
http://mrschureads.blogspot.com

Mr. Schu is a former school librarian who is now a part-time lecturer at Rutgers University. Mr. Schu is also the Ambassador of School Libraries for Scholastic.

10. Writing for Kids (While Raising Them) by Tara Lazar
http://taralazar.com
Tara Lazar writes this blog about children's literature. She writes humorous picture books.

11. Multicultural Children's Book Day
http://multiculturalchildrensbookday.com/blog
Children's reading advocates Valarie Budayr and Mia Wenjen team up to write about children's literature from a mom's perspective.

12. Kids Talk Kid Lit: What Kids Are Saying about the Books They're Reading
http://strohreads.blogspot.com
Kurt Stroh is a K–4 teacher-librarian who loves connecting kids to books.

13. Books 4 Your Kids
http://books4yourkids.com
Tanya Turek is a mother who worked in the bookseller industry. She is now an elementary school librarian. She is an avid reader of children's literature

14. Read It Daddy: Books, Comics and Cool Stuff for Kids!
http://readitdaddy.blogspot.com
Father and daughter team up to read and review children's books.

15. Barnes & Noble: The B&N Kids Blog
http://barnesandnoble.com/blog/kids
Major bookseller Barnes & Noble blogs about all things children's literature.

16. ALSC Blog: Pursuing Excellence for Library Service to Children
http://alsc.ala.org/blog
The blog of the Association for Library Service to Children (ALSC). Members of ALSC are guest bloggers.

17. Lovereading4Kids Blog
http://blog.lovereading4kids.co.uk
This blog was created by a team of "avid bookworms" who wanted to share their book recommendations with parents.

18. Pratham Books
http://blog.prathambooks.org
Pratham Books is a nonprofit publisher specializing in children's books in India.

19. Nosy Crow Blog
http://nosycrow.com/blog
Nosy Crow is an independent children's book and app publisher. They specialize in "child-focused, parent-friendly" books.

20. Children's Book Academy
http://childrensbookacademy.com/blog
The Children's Book Academy began in 2012 as a site to learn about writing for children. Mira Reisberg was the founding member.

21. Colours of Us
http://coloursofus.com/
Blog written by Svenja who is an adopted mother and social worker who is living in South Africa. She features multicultural books.

22. Charlesbridge: Children's Books Blog
http://charlesbridge.com/blogs/news
The blog of Charlesbridge Children's Books publisher.

23. Read Kid Do Read: Dedicated to Making Kids Readers for Life
http://readkiddoread.com/blog
Author James Patterson's blog. In addition to his own children's books, there are also reviews of books from other authors.

24. Picturebook Makers
http://blog.picturebookmakers.com
The blog is primarily about the artists who illustrate picture books.

25. Seven Impossible Things before Breakfast
http://blaine.org/sevenimpossiblethings/Playing By the Book
The blog began in 2006 as a book review blog. It has evolved but still publishes reviews and concentrates mainly on picture books.

26. Playing by the Book
http://playingbythebook.net
Zoe Toft began the blog in 2009. She publishes reviews of children's books.

27. Jump into a Book
http://jumpintoabook.com
The title of this blog uses the illusion of jumping into a book and getting lost in a good story.

28. Storytime Magazine: Classic Stories for Kids to Read, Love, and Share
http://storytimemagazine.com/news
Subscribe to the Storytime blog to read stories for kids and reading for pleasure.

29. Orange Marmalade: Spreading the Word on Delightful Children's Literature
http://orangemarmaladebooks.com
The blog has been focusing on middle grade fiction dealing with refugees and asylum seekers.

30. Children's Books Daily: Daily Reading from the Daley Household
http://childrensbooksdaily.com
Written by Megan Daley, the blog is about all things literary.

31. Fundamental Children's Books
http://itsfundamental.info
Crystal began her blog to help homeschoolers find good books.

32. KidLit411
http://www.kidlit411.com
The goal of the blog is to be a "one stop information shop for children's writers and illustrators."

33. Barrington Stoke: Cracking Reading for Over a Decade
http://barringtonstoke.co.uk/blog
Barrington Stoke was founded by Patience Thomson and Lucy Juckes to serve kids with dyslexia. They use dyslexia-friendly font and tinted paper. Their blog highlights new books as well as information about dyslexia.

34. Muslim Children's Books
http://muslimchildrensbooks.co.uk/blog
Based in the United Kingdom, Muslim Children's Books publishes books geared to children to inspire a love of Allah.

35. The Book Chook
http://thebookchook.com

Australian Susan Stephenson reviews books for primary school students.

36. The Brown Bookshelf
http://thebrownbookshelf.com
The Brown Bookshelf is intended to "push awareness of the myriad Black voices writing for young readers."

37. Randomly Reading: A Blog Reviewing Children's, Young Adult, and Adult Books
http://randomlyreading.blogspot.com
The author of this blog describes it as a "smorgasbord, a literary buffet." There are reviews for children of all ages.

38. Picture Books Blogger by Sarah Yewman
http://picturebooksblogger.wordpress.com
Sarah Yewman blogs about her opinions on picture books old and new.

39. Becky's Book Reviews
http://blbooks.blogspot.com
Becky is an avid reader and writes reviews for those books. The blog is not limited to children's books, and adult books are included.

40. Federation of Children's Book Groups
http://fcbg.org.uk/blog
This blog is maintained by the Federation of Children's Book Groups, which is a charity in the United Kingdom that encourages reading for pleasure.

41. KidLit Reviews: Honest, Thoughtful Reviews
http://kid-lit-reviews.com
This blog is written by Suzanne Morris. She has been reviewing kids' books for a long time.

42. Jabber Works by Sarah McIntyre
http://jabberworks.livejournal.com
The blog of author/illustrator Sarah McIntyre.

43. Story Snug: Children's Books and Learning Activities
http://storysnug.com
Catherine describes her blog as book recommendations rather than reviews. She is a mom living and writing in Germany.

44. Poetry for Children
http://poetryforchildren.blogspot.com
Sylvia Vardell is an author who writes the blog. Her emphasis is poetry for children.

45. Great Kid Books
http://greatkidbooks.blogspot.com
Mary Ann Scheuer is a school librarian who blogs about children's books.

46. This Kid Reviews Books by Erik
http://thiskidreviewsbooks.com
Erik is a kid who loves books. He blogs about those he has read and gives his opinion of the age appropriateness of the title.

47. Monica Edinger
http://medinger.wordpress.com
Author Monica Edinger began the blog to write about teaching. She now includes information about books for children.

48. Magination Press
http://maginationpress.apabooks.org
Magination Press is a book publisher that publishes books from the American Psychological Association.

49. Children's Books Heal
http://childrensbooksheal.com
Patricia Titlton is a children's author. Her blog features books from many authors.

50. Joan Holub
http://joanholub.com/news
Well-known author Joan Holub has written and illustrated more than 150 books. She blogs about her books and writing in general.

51. What to Read to Your Kids
http://whattoreadtoyourkids.com
Melissa LaSalle is a mother who is passionate about reading. She gives recommendations for what to read with your child.

52. My Book Corner
http://mybookcorner.co.uk

My Book Corner is written by a team of published authors, teachers, and more. They offer recommendations for good reading.

53. Mundie Kids Children's Book Review Blog
http://mundiekids.blogspot.com
This blog is written by the Mundie Moms, a group of moms who come together to look at books for ages 0–12.

54. Flowering Minds: Children's Book Review Site
http://floweringminds.wordpress.com
The Flowering Minds reviews mainly picture books with South Asian influence.

55. Big Book Little Book
http://bigbooklittlebook.com
From the United Kingdom, this blog is written by moms and their kids.

56. Addison Reads
http://addisonreads.com/posts
Addison Reads began in 2016 as a way to share and categorize the books Addison read to her daughter. She gives ideas for building an intentional children's book shelf.

57. Marble Spark
http://marblespark.com/blog
Marble Spark is written by parents for parents. They don't limit themselves to books but do offer personalized books for your children.

58. Minerva Reads: Kid's Books: Thoughts, Recommendations, and Reviews
http://minervareads.com
A writer, children's reading consultant, and freelance editor puts together thoughts on children's books and reviews.

59. Picture Book Den
http://picturebookden.blogspot.com
This blog features reviews on picture books and illustrators.

60. Butterfly Books
http://butterflychildrensbooks.com/blog
Written by a Canadian mom and lifelong lover of books. It is also a subscription service where you can receive books throughout the year.

61. The Picture Book Review
http://thepicturebookreview.com
This stay-at-home mom started this blog as a way to connect with others to talk about picture books.

62. Raise Them Righteous
http://raisethemrighteous.wordpress.com
Children's picture book reviews from the left.

63. The Nonfiction Detectives
http://nonfictiondetectives.com
Two librarians review nonfiction books for children.

64. A Kids Book a Day: Reviewing a Children's Book from 2017 Every Day
http://kidsbookaday.com
Librarian Janet Dawson posts a review each day.

65. Bobs Books Blog
http://bobsbooksnz.wordpress.com
Bob is a children's literature expert from New Zealand. He spent many years at the National Library of New Zealand selecting fiction and picture books for school libraries.

66. Sarah Webb
http://sarahwebb.info/blog
Sarah Webb is an award-winning children's author. Here she shares her favorite children's books.

67. Books for Kids Blog by GTG
http://booksforkidsblog.blogspot.com
Written by a librarian, this blog reviews books for kids from preschool to high school.

68. Alli Brydon Creative: Children's Book Editor
http://allibrydon.com/blog
An independent children's book editorial business. Offers advice and information about children's books.

69. SCBWI Australia East and New Zealand Blog
http://scbwiaustralianz.com
This blog is maintained by the Society of Children's Book Writers and Illustrators of Australia and New Zealand.

70. Vivian Kirkfield
http://viviankirkfield.com
Vivian Kirkfield is a children's book author who blogs about all things picture books.

71. 2 Kids and Tired Books: Books I've Read. Some I Recommend. Some I Don't.
http://2kidsandtiredbooks.blogspot.com
A tired mom living in Idaho who writes about books she has read.

72. Library Mice: Reviews from a Children's Book Enthusiast
http://librarymice.com
From a school librarian and mum in the United Kingdom. Emphasis on picture books.

73. Kid Lit Frenzy
http://kidlitfrenzy.com/kid-lit-frenzy
Alyson Beecher is an educator and book geek. She blogs about children's books for all ages.

74. The Overflowing Library
http://overflowinglibrary.com
This blog was started to keep track of the books that Kirsty read. She has expanded the site and is now overflowing with reviews.

75. Through the Looking Glass Book Review
http://lookingglassreview.blogspot.com
Books reviews, interviews with authors, and other topics dealing with children's literature.

76. Bridget and the Books
http://bridgetandthebooks.com
Bridget is an elementary school student.

77. Charlotte's Library
http://charlotteslibrary.blogspot.com
Charlotte concentrates on children's fantasy and science fiction books.

78. Wild Rose Reader
http://wildrosereader.blogspot.com
Elaine Magliarois a former elementary teacher and librarian. She has also taught children's literature at the college level.

79. Books4Learning
http://books4learning.blogspot.com
A teacher at all levels, this college English instructor blogs about children's books.

80. Did You Ever Stop to Think
http://didyoueverstoptothink.wordpress.com
From the United Kingdom, this blog has reviews about children's literature, graphic novels, and other bookish things.

81. Under the Guava Tree
http://underthatguavatree.com
Children's book reviews, stories, fables, and more.

82. Young Readers: Where Books and Babies Mix and Mingle
http://zero-to-eight.blogspot.com
This blog is intended to give reviews that parents, grandparents, and book lovers of all ages can enjoy.

83. The CWILLBC Society Blog
http://cwillbc.wordpress.com
This is the official blog of the CWILLBC (Children's Writers and Illustrators of British Columbia).

84. Children's War Books
http://childrenswarbooks.blogspot.com
From New Zealand, this blog concentrates on children's books dealing with war.

85. Book Lover Jo
http://bookloverjo.wordpress.com
A primary school librarian and obsessed with children's books. Mainly writes about primary fiction.

86. Book Monsters: Sink Your Teeth into a Great Book!
http://bookmonsters.info/blog
Ally's Book Monster will help you sniff out a good book.

87. The Write Path
http://dorinewhite.blogspot.com
Dorine White is an author who keeps a blog about books.

88. Bookworm for Kids
http://bookwormforkids.blogspot.com
Reviews of children's books from toddler to teen.

89. Only Picture Books
http://onlypicturebooks.com

As the name implies, this blog is about picture books. In addition to picture book reviews, there are interviews and educational activities.

90. Gecko Press
http://geckopress.com/blog

Gecko Press in an independent publisher in New Zealand. They translate and publish a small number of books from other countries.

91. Wanda Luthman's Children's Books
http://wandaluthman.wordpress.com

Author Wanda Luthman blogs about books that encourage good behavior in quality literature.

92. Book Bairn and the Wee Page Turner
http://bookbairn.blogspot.com

From Scotland, a mum writes about what she and her children like to read.

93. Hygge Stories: Children's Book Reviews
http://hyggestories.ca/kids-books-blog

The word Hygge (pronounced "hoo-gah") means coziness. This blog seeks out quality stories with great illustrations.

94. Booktalks—Quick and Simple Blog
http://booktalker.blogspot.com

The companion blog to Booktalks—Quick and Simple website, the blog publishes book talks for thousands of books. The website publishes a book talk a day.

95. Curious City: Children's Book Marketing Projects and Reviews
http://curiouscity.net/blog

Kirsten Cappy blogs about all things children's literature.

96. Childtastic Books: Great Books for Great Readers
http://childtasticbooks.wordpress.com

From the United Kingdom, this blog is run by a mom and daughter duo.

97. SDSU Children's Literature Blog
http://sdsuchildlit.blogspot.com

From the San Diego ChildLit Grad Student Association at SDSU.

98. CbM Author and Illustrator
http://www.cbmauthor.com
CbM is an author and illustrator. Not all the books she blogs about are geared to children.

99. The Kiddosphere@Fauquier
http://kiddosphere.blogspot.com
Blogs about children's and YA books. There are some adult fiction and nonfiction included as well.

100. Everything Children's Literature
http://everythingchildrenslit.blogspot.com
Janna from Connecticut blogs about children's books she has read.

Social Networking

Social networking allows users with similar interests to interact. Social networks can use apps or web pages to connect with others who use the same app. Contacts are created through people signing up to use the site and then "friending" other users. There are many different social networks that use different features. Users can share text, videos, photos, or links to other sites. The social media app chosen depends on what it will be used for. Over 80 percent of Americans belong to at least one social media site.

There are hundreds of uses for social networking in education. Libraries can use social media for a variety of book promotion activities. Here are some ideas for using social networking in book promotion:

- Share pictures of books and authors.
- Highlight services of a library.
- Highlight collections of books.
- Showcase books newly added to collection.
- Show books in pop culture.
- Live streaming of book chats.

Here are examples of social media that can be used in book promotion:

Facebook
http://www.facebook.com

Facebook has been around since 2004. Used by individuals initially, Facebook has emerged as an important advertising platform. Most libraries and schools have a Facebook presence that can connect with users.

If you do not have a Facebook page, you should. It is easy to set up the page and to add posts. To create a Facebook page:

- Go to http://www.facebook.com/pages.
- Click on Create Page.
- Choose local business or place.
- Choose library (or other appropriate designation).
- Click Add Info, Get Started.
- Add content.
  - Add image.
  - Add basic information about your institution.
  - You can add hours of operation if appropriate.
  - Add a description of your institution.
  - Add e-mail, phone number, and URL of website.
  - Save.
- View your site to be sure it looks as you want.
- "Like" your page. This will notify contacts that your page is available.
- Recommend your page to friends.
- Add your first post.

The Facebook page does not have to be limited to book promotion. Anything that is going on that you want your users to know can be posted on the page.

Here are promotion ideas for your Facebook page:

- Book talks
- Links to YouTube book trailers
- Highlighting new books
- Photos from around the library that show books: displays, hold shelf, book checkout, etc.
- Facebook live for book promotions
- Author events

Twitter
http://www.twitter.com

Twitter is an online social network that allows quick communication. It is a microblogging platform that limits users to 280 characters per tweet. It is useful for short bursts of communication.

Set up an account:

- Sign up using e-mail or phone number.
- Choose a profile name. If you are using multiple social media platforms, you may wish to use the same username on each to help your users find you on various sites.
- Add a photo.
- Complete your biography. Limited to 160 characters. The biography tells everyone who you are (e.g., public library, schoolteacher)
- Add website address. Or you can link to other social media sites.
- Follow a few similar twitter accounts
- Start tweeting.

Be sure to check your feed regularly to keep material fresh and interact with others.

There are many uses for Twitter in book promotion:

- Post reviews of books.
- Post news of new book arrivals.
- Interact with authors.
- Create Twitter chats. You can designate a particular time for your chat and create a hashtag. Users can log in during that time and use the hashtag to contribute to the chat. Users search for the hashtag to follow the chat.
- Similarly, create online book clubs.

Pinterest
http://www/pinterest.com

Pinterest is a virtual pin board where you can pin images from other sites that will link back to the original site. Others can re-pin images to their own boards. Pinterest is used by more than 250 million people with 175 billion items on 3 billion boards. Pinterest is used by a great many people for many interests. Since you can have several boards on your site, you can organize your site to save a variety of information.

To set up a Pinterest account:

- Go to http:www.pinterest.com.
- Sign up.
- You can link to your Facebook or Twitter accounts if you wish.

- Create profile and username. If you use several social media sites, you may wish to use the same username on each to help your followers find you.
- Choose the settings you wish. You can be notified when someone re-pins from your board.

To pin to your board:

- Install Pin button on your web browser or locate the Pin-it button on the page you are viewing.
- To pin, click on pin button. A screen will pop up to allow you to choose image to pin and choose which board to use. You can also create a new board from the dropdown menu.
- To create a new board, click the add button. Select the option to Create a new board. Name the board and select the category.
- To re-pin from other boards, hover over the image until you see three dots. Click Re-pin.

Pinterest can be used for a great many reading promotions. You can create boards for different genres. New books can be showcased. Author websites can be linked.

Authors have been using Pinterest to promote their works. They can have idea boards, book boards, etc.

Publishers use Pinterest to promote their books. You can re-pin to your board.

Some YA authors who use Pinterest include:

Laurie Halse Anderson
http://www.pinterest.com/halseanderson
Author of many YA books, Anderson has several boards that give readers a look into projects she is working on.

Leigh Bardugo
http://www.pinterest.com/lbardugo
Author of the *Six of Crows* and the *Grisha Trilogy*, Bardugo maintains several boards that help her readers plunge into her fantasy world.

Kami Garcia
http://www.pinterest.com/kamigarcia
Best-selling author of *Beautiful Creature*, Kami Garcia has different boards for each of her books. See how she gets her ideas and how the books develop.

Sarah J. Maas
http://www.pinterest.com/sarahjmaas
Teen favorite Sarah J. Maas, author of the *Throne of Glass* series, has create boards to go along with her series.

Marissa Meyer
http://www.pinterest.com/marissameyer22
Author of the *Lunar Chronicles* and *Heartless* offers a glimpse of her process by the pins on her boards.

Jennifer Niven
http://www.pinterest.com/allbrightplaces
Author of *All the Bright Places*, Jennifer Niven shares her travels and inspirations through her Pinterest boards.

James Patterson
http://www.pinterest.com/jamespatterson1
Kids' favorite author, James Patterson, maintains several boards including ones for his series books.

Beth Revis
http://www.pinterest.com/bethrevis
Author of *Across the Universe*, she has boards on her books and writing process as well as boards on crafts she enjoys.

Michael Scott
http://www.pinterest.com/flamelauthor
Author of the *Secrets of the Immortal Nicholas Flamel* has several boards that showcase his series books and his writing process.

Tumblr
http://www.tumblr.com

Tumblr is a microblogging platform. Users can add small snippets of information, videos, images, etc. It is a fast and easy app that is used by more than 176 million users.

To set up an account:

* Enter e-mail address and choose a username and password. If you use multiple social sites, you may want to use the same username on each so user can find you easily.

- Click Sign Up.
- You will be asked your age to ensure you are over 13. Tumblr is used frequently by teens.
- Check Agree to Terms.
- Click Done.
- You will be asked to list three blogs to follow. You can search by key word to find similar Tumblr sites.
- Set up background image, profile image, title, and description.
- Click Make It.
- You will be sent an e-mail to verify your account.
- Start Tumbling.

Here are ideas for using Tumblr in book promotion:

- Link to book talks and book trailers.
- Link to author sites.
- Videos of new books.
- Photos of book displays.

Instagram

Instagram is a popular photo-sharing app used by more than 80 million people. It allows you to use filters and special effects to enhance your photos.
Instagram is easy to set up:

- Download the app onto your device.
- Choose username and password. If you are using multiple social media sites, you may want to use the same username on the site so followers can find you easily.
- Write your biography.
- Add your organization URL.

Posting to Instagram:

- Open Instagram.
- You can take a picture using the picture icon or upload from your camera roll.
- Tap the icon on the bottom of the screen.
- Once you have the photo, you can add effects, filters, captions, and/or location.
- Click on Share.

There are many ways to use Instagram for book promotion:

- Show off your books.
- Show unboxing of new books to give a sneak peek at new books.
- Show the book-processing activity.
- Highlight book author events.
- Take pictures of print marketing to digitize it.
- Throwback days to highlight older books.

Goodreads
http://www.goodreads.com

Web based, iOS, Android.

Goodreads is a social networking site for people who love books. It is a good place to have an online book club. Share what you are reading and make suggestions for your patrons.

To use Goodreads:

- Create an account using your e-mail address.
- Select favorite genres.
- Click Continue.
- The site will automatically give you suggestions for books you may like.
- You will have "shelves" for you to place your books. You can rate the books or place them on the Want to Read shelf or the Read shelf.
- You can search for more books to add to your account.
- Click on the book cover to select the book to Rate It or Review It. Once you review the book, add the date and save.

In addition to the built-in shelves in Goodreads, you can create your own shelves. Once a book is placed on a customized shelf, it cannot be on any other shelves. To create your own shelf:

- Go to My Books.
- Click on Edit Shelves.
- Click Add Shelf.
- Add a title for the new shelf. Shelves can be by genre, themes, classes, or any other purpose you have.

After shelf is created and books have been added, you can share the shelf on your web page of social media by creating a widget.

To create a widget:

- Go to My Books.
- Click on Widgets.
- Click on Customize Your Widget.
- Select shelf to share.
- Add title.
- The embed code will be created.
- Copy embed code, and add to your web page or social media site.

Having a Good Reads widget on your page is a good way to advertise books that you want to showcase. You can have multiple shelves to share on a variety of sites. Create a shelf for state book award nominees. Create a shelf for holiday books. Create a shelf for local authors. Anything you can image can be used.

If This Then That
http://ifttt.com

If This Then That (IFTTT) is a great tool to use if you want to add content on several social media sites at once. IFTTT allows you to connect your accounts and content to be able to publish once and have your content pushed out on other accounts. For instance, suppose you want to publish a book suggestion as a blog post. Using IFTTT, you can automatically have that blog post shared on Twitter. You can share on several sites at once. In addition to connecting apps, IFTTT also allows you to control the IoT, which will allow you to control your lights with your smartphone. Or log your calls into a spreadsheet. If you can dream it, you will probably be able to create an applet to do it in IFTTT.

The first step is to create an account in IFTTT. You can use your Google account or your Facebook account.

There are many applets that can be created. You can look through the existing recipes to see examples of what others have been done. If you see something you want to use, you can use it as your own. IFTTT will step you through applying the applet to your accounts.

To build an applet, simply fill in the dialog box.

- Build new applet.
- New applet.

- If _____, choose it. You can search through the apps that can be used.
- Choose trigger.
- Then _____, choose it.
- Choose action.

An example of a simple applet you can create is:

If there is a new post on my blog, then publish it on Twitter. You will be asked your login information for the accounts, so the actions can be completed.

Other examples of what you can do:

Tweet your Instagram as a photo on Twitter.

Blog your Twitter feed.

Post Instagram photos to Tumbler.

IFTTT is a real-time saver if you want to publish on multiple sites. It allows you to have a wide presence without spending a great deal of time.

Children's Authors to Follow on Twitter

There are many authors who use Twitter to keep their fans up to date on what is going on in their author world. Twitter is a good platform since tweets are limited to 280 characters and can be written on the fly. Twitter streams can be embedded into web pages, so you can share with your children what their favorite author is writing.

Some of the most popular children's authors to follow include:

Alan Gratz @Alan_Gratz

Anthony Horowitz @AnthonyHorowitz

Barry Lyga @barrylyga

Coe Booth @coebooth

Dana Reinhardt @dsreinhardt

E. Lockhart @elockhart

Ellen Hopkins @EllenHopkinsYA

Eoin Colfer @eoincolfer

Gordon Korman @gordonkorman

Holly Black @hollyblack

Jeff Kinney @wimpykid

Jennifer Holm @jenniholm

Jenny Han @jennyhan

J. K. Rowling @jk_rowling

Jo Knowles @joknowles

John Green @johngreen

Judy Blume @judyblume

K. L. Going @klgoing

Karma Wilson @KarmaWilson

Kate Messner @kmessner

Laurie Halse Anderson @halseanderson

Libba Bray @libbabray

Lisa McMann @lisa_mcmann

Marie Lu @Marie_Lu

Maureen Johnson @maureenjohnson

Meg Cabot @megcabot

Michael Rosen @MichaelRosenYes

Mitali Perkins @mitaliperkins

Mo Willems @The_Pigeon

Neil Gaiman @neilhimself

Oliver Jeffers @OliverJeffers

R. L. Stine @RL_Stine

Rachel Renee Russell @DorkDiaries

Raina Telegemeir @goraina

R. J. Palacio @RJPalacio

Sara Zarr @sarazarr

Sarah Dessen @sarahdessen

Authors Who Skype

Author visits are a marvelous way to get children excited about reading and books. You only have to watch the children's faces when they are listening to an author to know the magical effect it has on them.

When a face-to-face author visit is not available, you can still bring authors into your classroom or library using technology. Virtual author visits are a great way to introduce children to an author. There are many authors who are willing to Skype or Facetime into a classroom to meet the students. Many authors will agree to short Skype visits for no fee.

Once you have decided on who you want to invite, you will need to contact the author or their agent. Authors often have contact information for Skype visits on their web pages. Below there are links to sites that list authors who Skype or contacts.

You will need to prepare for the Skype visit. Authors may be taking time out of their writing time to participate, so you don't want to have to deal with technical issues on their time if you can help it. Being prepared is the best time saver. Ask if the author will begin with a presentation, a reading, or just answer questions.

Preparing for the visit:

Technology:

- Install Skype or Facetime on a dependable computer. Be sure to ask the author which platform works best for them.
- Be sure you have a good Internet connection that will be used for streaming audio and video.
- You may want to ask others on your network to refrain from high band use activities during the time you are hosting the author.
- Connect the computer to a projector and screen so the video can be seen by everyone. Attach speakers so the author can be heard. Don't rely on built-in speakers.
- You will need a microphone if the visit will include questions from the children.
- Create a Skype account and connect your account to the author's account.
- Test your Skype account by testing on another Skype user using the same equipment you will be using the day of the author visit.
- Some authors like to connect a few minutes before the scheduled start to be sure everything works. Don't be discouraged if it doesn't. Hang up and try again.

Preparing children for the visit:

- As with any author visit, the children should be prepared before the start of the visit.
- Children should be familiar with the author's work. The book could be one you have shared or will share with the children.
- Look at the author's website and familiarize the children with available materials.
- Download any activity guides provided.
- Children should be prepared with questions they would like to ask. If there are time restraints, choose which children will be asking the questions.

- Students should be polite and pay attention during the visit. Remember, the video goes two ways, and the author will be able to see if children are not paying attention.
- After the visit, encourage the children to write thank you cards or pictures to the author to show them how much the children appreciate the time the author gave.

Candlewick Press in Your Classroom
http://education.microsoft.com/candlewick

Kate Messner's Authors Who Skype with Classes and Book Clubs (for Free!)
http://www.katemessner.com/authors-who-skype-with-classes-book -clubs-for-free

Penguin Authors
http://www.penguin.com/school-library/skype-authors

Scholastic Skype in the Classroom
http://education.microsoft.com/scholastic

World Read Aloud Day
http://education.microsoft.com/WRAD

YA Books and More Authors Who Skype (or Have Skyped)
http://naomibates blogspot.com/p/authors-who-skype-or-have-skyped.html

Nonfiction Resources

Not all children like to read fiction books. When preparing book promotion activities, don't forget good nonfiction books. To find lists of nonfiction books that you may want to promote, you can use these resources:

AAAS/Subaru SB&F Prizes for Excellence in Science Books
http://www.sbfprize.org
This award recognizes excellence in nonfiction science books for children and young adults.

Boston Globe–Horn Book Awards
http://www.hbook.com/boston-globe-horn-book-awards
The Boston Globe–Horn Book Awards are given annually in the categories of Picture Book, Fiction and Poetry, and Nonfiction.

Carter G. Woodson Book Awards—National Council for the Social Studies
http://www.socialstudies.org/awards/woodson
The Carter G. Woodson Book Award is presented to exemplary books written for children and young people.

Children's Book Guild Nonfiction Award
http://www.childrensbookguild.org/nonfiction-award/past-winners
This award is given annually to an author of nonfiction books whose works contribute to children's literature.

Giverny Award
http://www.15degreelab.com/givernyawarddescription.html
This award honors a children's science picture book written in the English language and published within five years of the award date. The book must teach its young reader at least one important scientific principle well or encourage the reader toward specific science-related attitudes, pursuits, or inquiries.

Golden Kite Awards
http://www.scbwi.org/awards/golden-kite-award
Given by the Society of Children's Book Writers and Illustrators. The Golden Kite Awards recognize excellence in children's literature in five categories: Young Reader and Middle Grade Fiction, Young Adult Fiction, Nonfiction, Picture Book Text, and Picture Book Illustration.

National Science Teachers Association Outstanding Science Trade Books for Students K–12
http://www.nsta.org/publications/ostb
Reading science trade books is the perfect way for students to build literacy skills while learning science content. The books that appear in these lists were selected as outstanding children's science trade books. They were chosen by a book review panel appointed by the National Science Teachers Association.

Orbis Pictus Award
http://www2.ncte.org/awards/orbis-pictus-award-nonfiction-for
-children
The Orbis Pictus Award is given by the National Council of Teachers of English recognizing excellence in the writing of nonfiction for children.

Robert F. Sibert Informational Book Medal
http://www.ala.org/alsc/awardsgrants/bookmedia/sibertmedal
Awarded annually to the author(s) and illustrator(s) of the most distinguished informational book published in the United States in English.

YALSA Excellence in Nonfiction for Young Adults—American Library Association
http://www.ala.org/awardsgrants/excellence-nonfiction-young-adults
In addition to awarding medals to the best fiction books, the American Library Association awards the Excellence in Nonfiction for Young Adults. This is an award for the best nonfiction book published for young adults (ages 12–18) during the November 1–October 31 publishing year.

Cloud Storage

When creating reading promotion materials for your program, you may find they take up a lot of storage room. You may not want to keep the files on your device and may want to use cloud storage to house the files. There are many cloud storage services that you can use. If you need a small amount storage, you will find many free sites that allow storage of 2 to 5 GB of files. If you need more than that, you can create multiple accounts or pay a small fee to upgrade your storage. Fees start at just $1 a month for some sites.

Google Drive: With each free google account, you get 15 GB of storage space included. You can add more storage. To add 100 GB of storage, the cost is $1.99.

Amazon Drive: Prime members receive free unlimited photo storage and 5 GB of video storage. 100 GB of storage for videos costs $11.99 a year.

pCloud: Offers 500 GB of storage for a one-time payment of $175.

Microsoft OneDrive: Free 5 GB of storage for registered users. Upgrade storage to 50 GB for $2 per month.

Apple iCloud: Included on all Apple devices. Allows 5 GB of free storage. To add storage, 50 GB costs $1 per month.

DropBox: Offers 2 GB free. Upgrade to 1 T for $8.25 per month.

Index

About the Author

NANCY J. KEANE is a retired school librarian. She has been a lover of children's literature all her life. Her earliest memories include walking to the public library and filling up her little red wagon with stories and adventures. Working with books and children is a perfect match for her. Nancy is the author of an award-winning website Booktalks—Quick and Simple (http://www.nancykeane.com/booktalks). The site has proven to be indispensable to librarians and teachers around the world. The database includes more than 10,000 ready-to-use book talks, and contributions are welcome from educators and students. Additionally, Nancy has a page of thematic book lists available on her page. *ATN Reading Lists* consists of more than 2,000 thematic lists culled from suggestions from several professional e-mail discussion lists and librarian suggestions. Nancy has written several professional books including *The Tech-Savvy Booktalker* and *101 Great, Ready-to-Use Book Lists for Teens*.

Nancy received a BA in psychology from the University of Massachusetts, Amherst, an MLS from the University of Rhode Island, an MA in educational technology from George Washington University, and an EdD in educational leadership from Rivier University. Nancy presents workshops and seminars on children's literature around the country. Nancy has won numerous awards for her work. She is currently a museum educator and shares stories of New Hampshire history to schoolchildren around the state. Nancy lives in New Hampshire and shares her home with an assortment of animals.